MANDALAS

*A Graphic
Prayer Book*

ISBN#: 978-1-936497-43-0
©2024, John G. Cunyus
All Rights Reserved
Art by John Cunyus

Searchlight Press
Who are you looking for?
Publishers of thoughtful Christian books since 1994.
5634 Ledgestone Drive
Dallas, TX 75214-2026
USA
www.JohnCunyus.com

Table of Contents

South Asian Traditions

Prayers and Meditations

Miscellaneous

Bibliography
About the Author

*"Truth is nobody's property;
no race, no individual can lay
any exclusive claim to it.
Truth is the nature of all souls."*

Vivekananda

Mandala

"A mandala is a geometric configuration of symbols. In various spiritual traditions, mandalas may be employed for focusing attention of practitioners and adepts, as a spiritual guidance tool, for establishing a sacred space and as an aid to meditation and trance induction."
Wikipedia

"Mandalas come in many forms."
The Asia Society

"1: a Hindu or Buddhist graphic symbol of the universe
specifically : a circle enclosing a square with a deity on each side that is used chiefly as an aid to meditation
2: a graphic and often symbolic pattern usually in the form of a circle divided into four separate sections or bearing a multiple projection of an image"
Merriam-Webster

**IS IT DANGEROUS TO MY CHRISTIAN SALVATION
TO READ THIS BOOK?**

In addition to Biblical themes, this work reflects on and adapts ancient South Asian prayer methods and images, as well as contemporary reflections by writers from those traditions. Is it dangerous to one's Christian salvation to be exposed to such things?

First of all, let me say I understand the question. I struggled with it intensely as a young man. <u>Nothing taught in the non-Christian sources used here is necessary to salvation</u>. **We are saved through Jesus Christ alone**. If you find yourself worrying excessively about whether to proceed, as a retired Pastor I encourage you not to. Take refuge in what you know to be true in Jesus, and leave it at that. I do not judge.

If you are inclined to go on and read, well and good. Let me share a few observations as you start the process.

First of all, no one knows exactly when the ancient sources included here were produced. South Asian society reckoned time differently than we do. The consensus of scholars I've encountered in my study suggests dates from 400 to 800 years before Christ for the Upanishads I have cited.

As such, they are not anti-Christian, un-Christian, or even non-Christian. They are pre-Christian, existing before Jesus was ever born on this Earth. These sources stand in the same relationship to Christ and His revelation as all other pre-Christian writings, including the Greek philosophical works. If we believe as St. Augustine did that "**All truth is God's truth**," then we can read such works with an open mind, informed by the Truth as revealed in Christ.

There are areas within ancient South Asian thought and its later interpretations that are incompatible with an orthodox Christian faith. In places, they imply pantheism or monism. This claims that God and the creation are ultimately one and the same.

This contradicts the Christian doctrine of Creation, which teaches that God makes the universe, but that the universe is not God. As my wife would instantly agree, I am not god. I have never been god. I'm convinced that no quantity of spiritual practice could ever turn me into god. Though my illustration is far too simple to do justice to the complexities of schools such as *Advaita Vedanta*, it gives us a rule of thumb as we proceed.

**What blurs or erases the line
between God and God's creation
is not acceptable from a Christian perspective.**

A biblical Christian cannot be a pantheist. Yet Swami Tyagisananda, a writer from whose commentaries I have drawn, avoids insisting that the pantheist position is the only one available. He outlines in depth both the pantheist position, which contradicts the Christian doctrine of creation, and the dualist position, which does not.

The particular dualist position described here is called panentheism in Western theology. It holds that God creates all and is in intimate relationship with all. Yet God remains God and the creation remains the creation. As the good Swami points out, when those who love God are absorbed in God's ecstatic love, the hair-splitting between pantheists and dualists becomes pointless. What matters is the love, bliss, and freedom poured out into the soul and into the world in that moment.

With that as a backdrop, there is much in the non-Christian sources that points directly to Christian understandings. *Svetasvatara Upanishad*, for instance, insists on the unity of God, behind the various forms the world worships.. *Chandogya Upanishad* affirms the Word as proceeding directly from God, and as forming the foundation of all that exists.

Narada's *Bhakti Sutras* insist that the human person cannot move toward God unless God makes it possible. We would have no idea of who God is, no clue as to where to seek, if God did not choose so. "Had it not been for God who guides the individual in his choice, he would not have been able to choose for himself," Tyagisananda says.

This foreshadows Paul's word in **1 Corinthians 12:3**: "*...no one can say, 'Jesus is Lord,' except by the Holy Spirit.*"

According to South Asian theologians, God's love fills the universe and makes life livable. God's love alone awakens the human soul. God's love draws us into a relationship that transforms. This points directly to John's word in **1 John 4:10**: "*In this is love, not that we have loved God but that he loved us and sent his Son to be the propitiation for our sins.*"

These sources in effect prophesy attributes of God that become manifest in the life, death, and Resurrection of Jesus Christ.

God's grace, the South Asians insist, underlies human liberation from beginning to end. Tyagisananda addresses the relationship between God's grace and the human response to it, saying, "A greater difficulty is as to how to reconcile the doctrine of grace with the doctrine of Karma or self-effort. Here also the difficulty can be overcome if we understand that the grace of God is bestowed on a person only after he has reached the limits of self-effort."

So, in this writer's opinion, a Christian can thoughtfully and prayerfully study these and other such pre-Christian works with an open mind and heart. As we do so, we keep in mind the primacy of the Gospel and work through areas where conflicts appear in light of it. Perhaps the best argument in favor is the sheer power of what is said. The following word has been most helpful me:

> "When a man knows God he is free.
> His sorrows have an end."

May it become so for all of us!

Amen.

How Can I Pray More Effectively?

1. Remember the link between breath and prayer, from **Genesis 2:7**. Repeat a verse from scripture or a prayer phrase for a specified number of breaths, to center yourself. When your mind wanders, bring it back.

2. Memorize certain prayers (the Lord's Prayer or the 23rd Psalm, for instance) to repeat when you're stressed.

3. Set an appointment to pray every day, then keep the appointment.

4. Find ways to integrate prayer into your "ordinary" activities.

The cumulative effect is a deepening sense of God's presence, through prayer. We can't command the lightning of God's power to strike. We can put up a lightning rod, though. Cultivating a sense of His presence is like putting up a lightning rod.

A Pattern for Prayer

Reflect on a passage from scripture or a piece of religious art. Let its meaning lead you into God's presence.

Praise God's greatness.

Ask God's forgiveness for your sins and offer your forgiveness to others for theirs. God has promised to forgive you as you forgive others.

Lift Up the needs of others. Be specific. Name names. Pray for the sick, the lost, your family, church, friends, and for the world.

Share your own concerns, holding nothing back. Clear your mind and heart. Ask for what you need. Be honest.

Give Thanks, whatever the situation may be. In Christ there is always light.

A Way of Meditative Prayer

1. Sit comfortably and breathe slowly and evenly, paying attention to each breath as it comes and goes. Again, see **Genesis 2:7**.

2. With each breath, repeat one of the prayer phrases in the book. When you find your mind wandering, gently bring your focus back to the breathing and prayer.

3. Set a timer and do this for five to ten minutes during the day, to center your soul on the God of scripture.

Biblical Traditions

Mandalas, 11

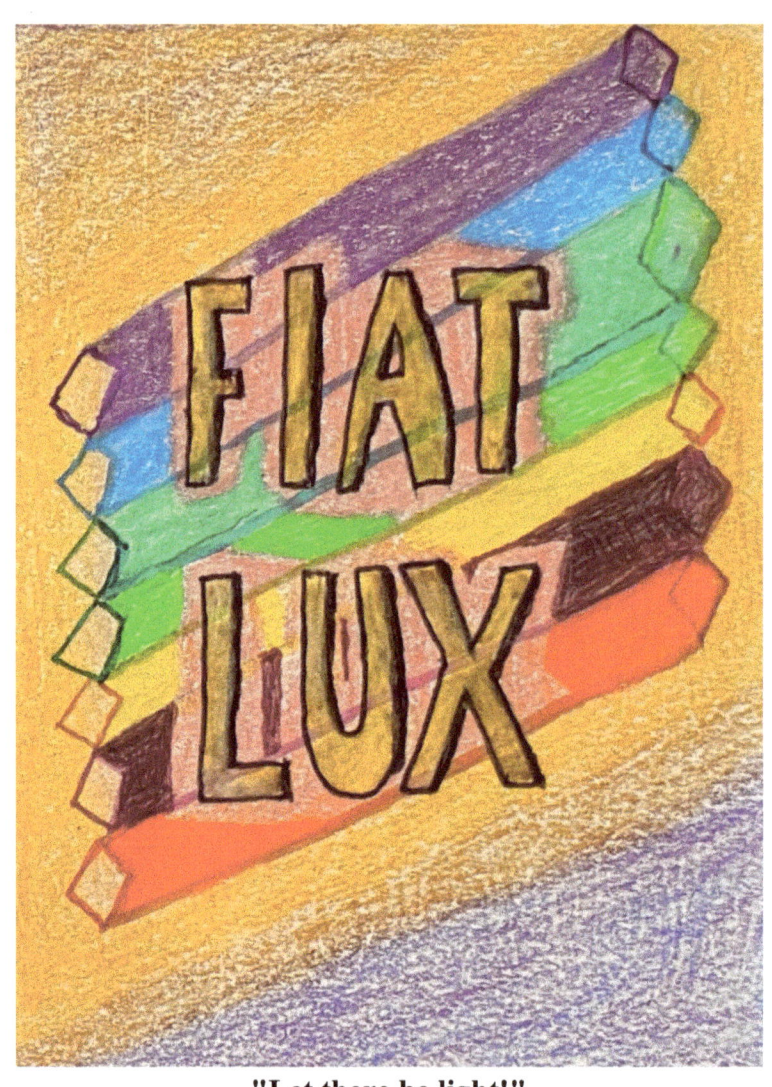

"Let there be light!"
Genesis 1:3

Mandalas, 12

1. "Fiat Lux"

In **Genesis 1:3**, the Lord says, "*Let there be light.*" In Latin, the phrase is, "*Fiat lux.*" The Hebrew original is transliterated as, "*Yehi or.*"

These words speak creation into being. The Word of God, identified in the New Testament as the *Logos*, begins to make all things manifest. Light comes first: not just physical light, but light in all its metaphorical connotations as well.

All of that begins with two words, according to the ancient texts.

The underlying Hebrew word for "created" implies an action that only God can do, and which has an excellent purpose in mind.

People ask, 'Is that literally true?' Yes, and more so!

When darkness weighs on you, remember those words.

"*Fiat lux.*"

"*Let there be light.*"

That's why you (and everything else) exist.

You don't have to find your purpose.

It will find you.

Mandalas, 13

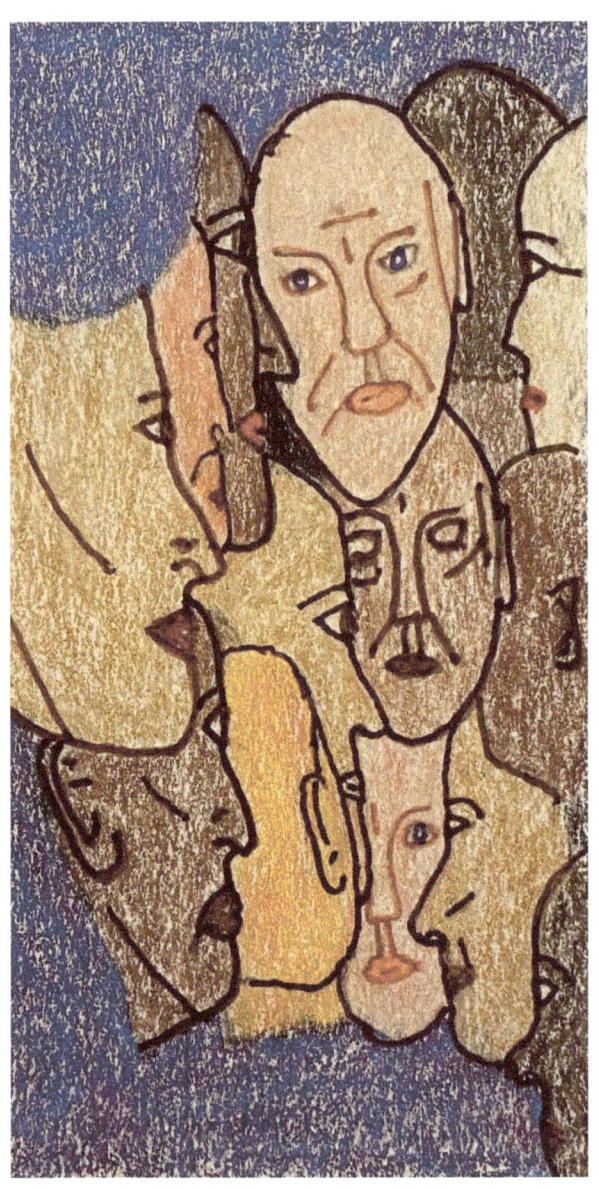

"The Human Family"
Acts 17:26

Mandalas, 14

2. "The Human Family"

The Apostle Paul, preaching publicly for the only recorded time in Athens, says in **Acts 17:26** that God *"...made from one every race of humanity to live on all earth's face."*

This echoes the teaching of Genesis. Humankind is no accident. Believe it or not, the original divine purpose of light finds its fullest expression in us.

Yet, look at the faces in this mandala! They all seem sad: no smiles, no apparent joy.

We seem to have stumbled on our way to becoming light.

Have we stumbled so as to fall, as Paul asks in **Romans 11:11**? Is our current sadness the last word? Not according to the unchanging purpose expressed in the previous mandala!

Could it be the sorrow into which all of us fall is merely the background against which we will measure the joy to come? Could God's purpose in us be greater than the misery around us?

Despair, written as it is all on so many faces, tempts us to answer no. The purpose has failed. Cynicism beckons. Yet the Biblical message says yes.

It's hard to believe in a godly purpose in the struggles of life! We all know that.

The only thing harder is ceasing to believe.

May God grant us the necessary courage!

Mandalas, 15

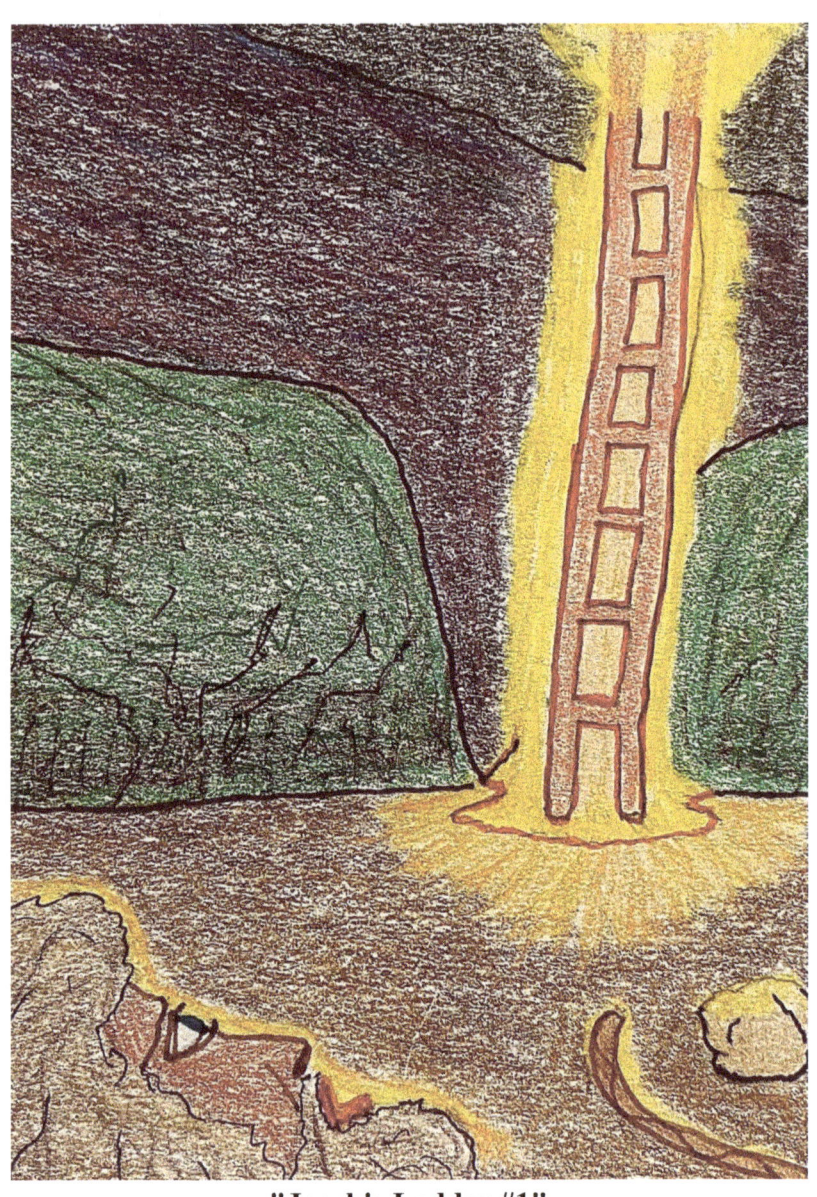

"Jacob's Ladder #1"
Genesis 28:12

Mandalas, 16

3. "Jacob's Ladder"

In **Genesis 28:12**, a man named Jacob flees from the anger of a brother determined to kill him. His very first night away from home, God gives Jacob a dream in which *"He saw in sleep a ladder standing on the ground, and its top touching the sky. God's angels likewise were climbing up and down by it."*

God shows Jacob at the beginning of his journey that heaven and earth are connected. There is a ladder. The divine and the human have a point of contact!

God gives Jacob this vision some 18 centuries before Christ. During the same epoch, South Asian sages 2500 miles to the East were painstakingly groping toward the same insight.

Ironically, Jacob does not climb up the ladder in this vision, nor does the Lord climb down. Both have other purposes at work at the time.

But there is a ladder! We are not cut off completely in our mortality! It falls to later generations to experience both the Lord's climbing down the ladder to live among us, and us taking our first, halting steps up the rungs of the ladder ourselves.

But remember: there is a ladder!

Mandalas, 17

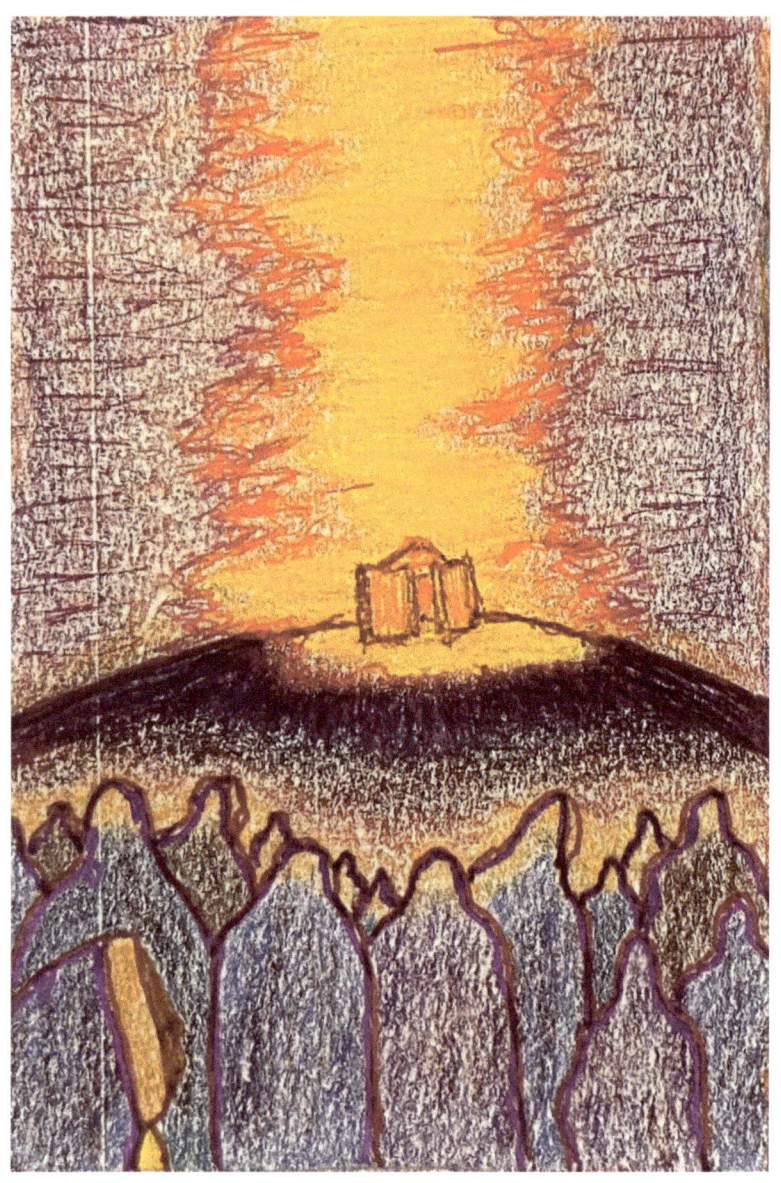

"The Pillar of Fire"
Exodus 13:21

Mandalas, 18

4. "The Pillar of Fire"

After God freed the people of Israel from Egyptian slavery, **Exodus 13:21** tells us, *"The Lord went before them to show the way, in a column of cloud by day and in a pillar of fire by night, so He could be Leader on the journey at both times."*

Imagine that!

God's people fell into slavery through hunger, hardship, and treachery. Those who posed as their benefactors became their slave-masters. In their suffering, Israel's children cried out to the Lord....and He HEARD them.

In this mandala, He leads them out of Egypt to the Mount of revelation, where He will give them the Law. He gives them the Law so they may keep the freedom He won for them.

Freedom in the Lord isn't doing whatever we want, whenever we want, to or with whomever we want. True freedom is living by the Ultimate, for the Ultimate, and ultimately with the Ultimate.

If we wander from that Pillar of Fire we wind up enslaved again, and the process must start over. How wonderful for us that the character of the Ultimate as absolute freedom never changes!

Nevertheless, we change unavoidably in this transient world. May our change always point us in the direction of the Ultimate.

Follow the fire!

Mandalas, 19

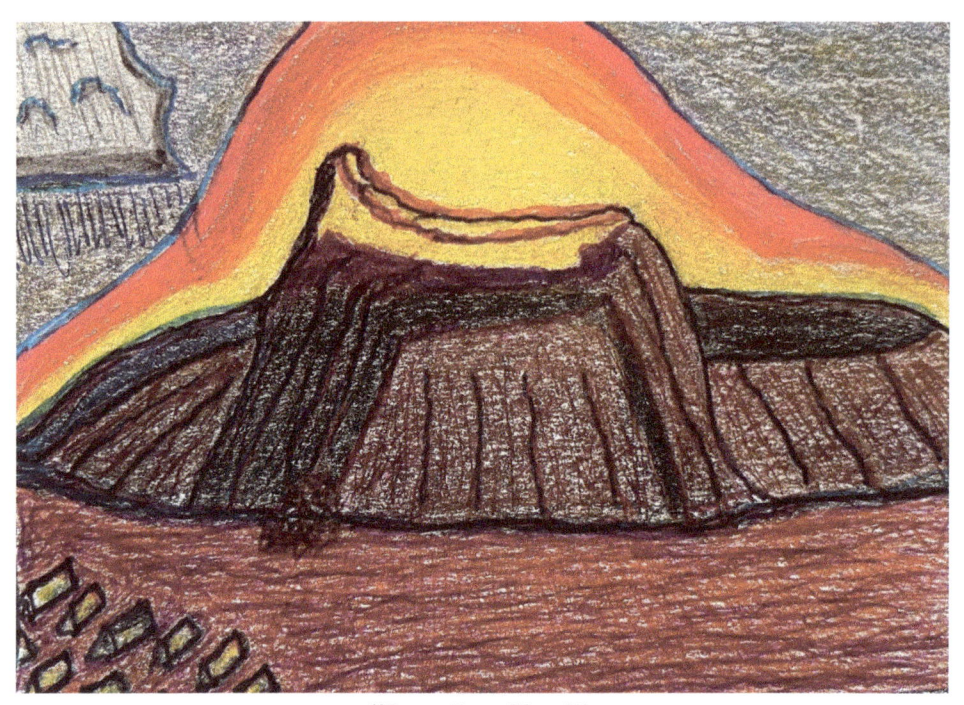

"Israel at Sinai"
Exodus 19:1-2

5. "Israel at Sinai"

Exodus 19:1-2 says, "*In the third month of Israel's going out of Egypt's land, they came on that day into Sinai's wasteland. Setting out from Raphidim and coming into Sinai's desert, they camped in the same place. Israel fixed tents out of the mountain region.*"

While there before Mount Sinai, stupendous miracles unfold before their eyes. The mountain itself shudders and burns from the weight of the divine presence.

On the third day, God Himself speaks to the people from the mountain, giving them the Ten Commandments. Overwhelmed with terror, they beg God through Moses not to speak to them again.

Moses climbs the mountain on their behalf. God reveals to him there the beginnings of the Law: the Holiness Code, and instructions for a place of worship.

Despite the overwhelming presence of God, the people turn away. When Moses delays coming down the mountain to them, they take matters into their own hands and make themselves "gods" of their own.

Sometimes even in moments that ought to be triumphs, we let fear overcome us. We turn away from the Ultimate, before whom we seem to ourselves to be nothing. We beg to hear no more. Afraid to make peace with the One who truly is, we settle for making our own "gods". We worship the works of our hands, rather than the One whose hands make us.

Have you ever turned away at the foot of the mountain?

What would it take to do otherwise?

Mandalas, 21

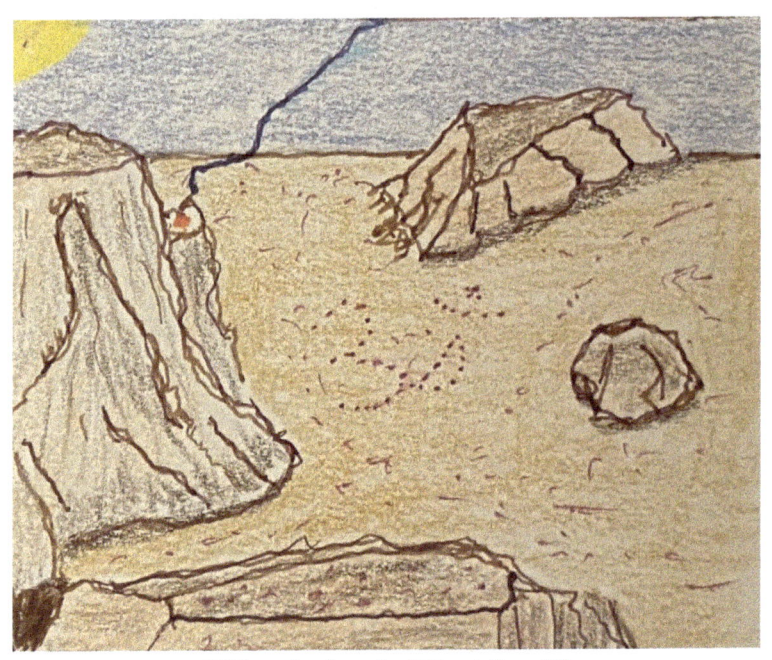

"Wandering in Wasteland"
Numbers 14:33

6. "Wandering in the Wasteland"

Disasters mount for Israel after its failure at Sinai. Moses pleaded with the Lord on their behalf, who forgave them and gave them further instruction. Then He commanded them to go up to the Promised Land.

Again, the people were afraid. Buying time, they sent twelve spies to scout the land they were to enter. When the spies returned, they described the land's bounty. Yet ten of the twelve told the people that the land's inhabitants were giants. They could not defeat such people, the ten said, and their children would end of being slaves to them.

Two of the twelve, Caleb and Joshua, urged a different course. Yes, the land's people were fearsome, they acknowledged. But surely the God who led us out of Egypt, fed us in the wasteland, and spoke to us at Sinai can lead us to victory again!

The people rebelled and refused to obey God's command. In response, the Lord tells them in **Numbers 14:33**, "*Your children will be wanderers in the desert for forty years.*"

The parents' disbelief causes consequences that their children have to bear. Yet those children never became slaves to giants in the Promised Land, as their anxious parents feared.

Sometimes disobedience and disbelief lead to our own long years of wandering. Yet even there, the Lord continues to reveal Himself. He does not abandon those He has freed, though their path grows longer through their own failure.

Even in the wasteland, even in the wandering, the Holy One is near.

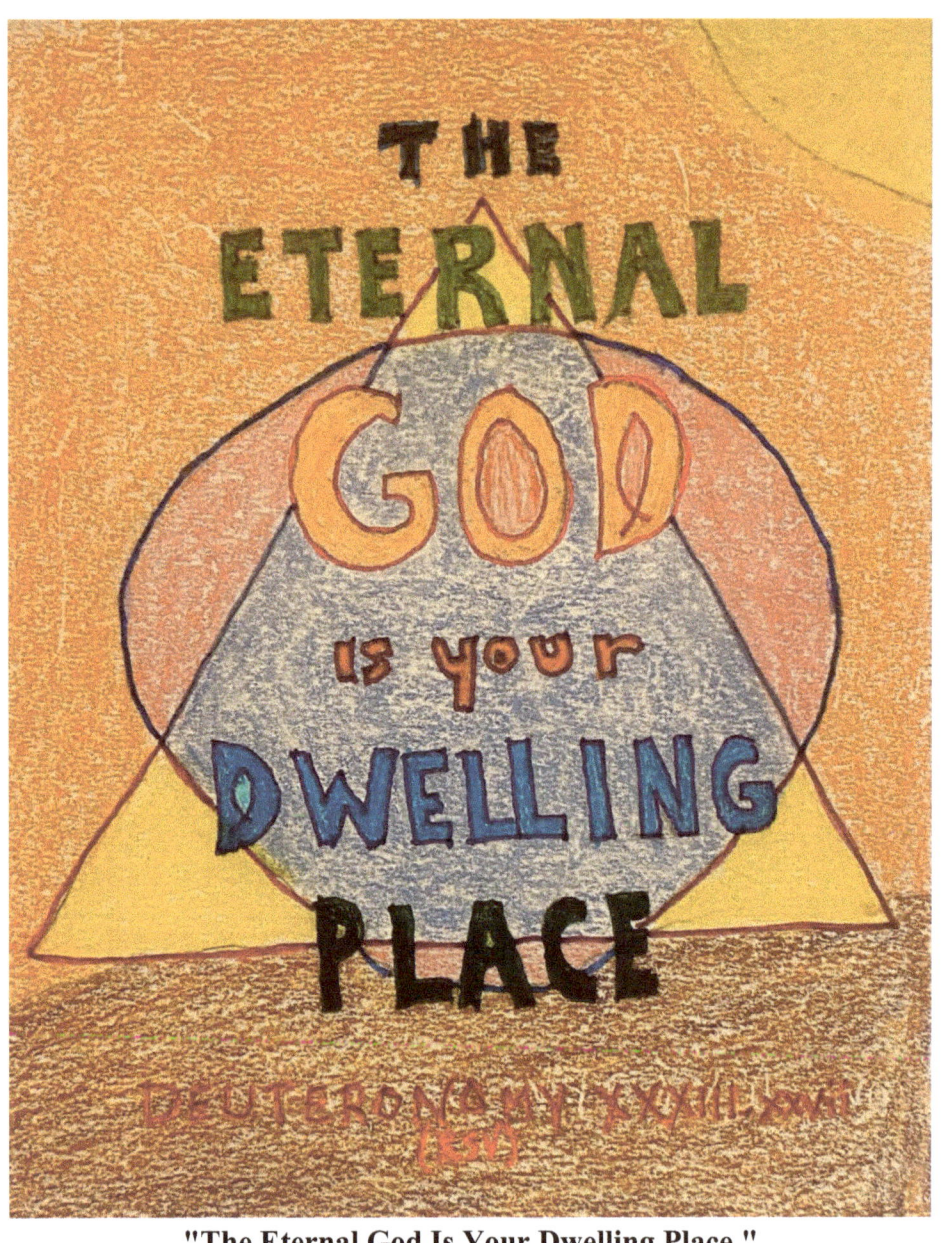

"The Eternal God Is Your Dwelling Place."
Deuteronomy 33:27 (RSV)

Mandalas, 24

7. "The Eternal God Is Your Dwelling Place."

Deuteronomy 33:27 in the Revised Standard Version of the Bible reads,

> *The eternal God is your dwelling place,*
> *and underneath are the everlasting arms.*

By the time Deuteronomy was written and the Torah completed, Israel had realized that no earthly land was an eternal possession. Instead, the nation's home was none other than the Ultimate, God Himself. All else fell apart, however glorious it might seem.

This realization was two-fold. On the one hand, Israel's national life and earthly existence had been scarred by struggle, disobedience, defeat, and exile. The permanent earthly kingdom once hoped for was seen to be a mirage, however important worldly justice and safety might be.

On the other hand, the one constant in their tumultuous existence had been the reality of the Lord at the heart of the people. Through highs and lows, births and deaths, victories and defeats, God, the Ultimate, continued with them.

Suffering and loss are unavoidable in this life. Yet our dwelling place as a people abides through it all. Can we direct our hearts to this as we make our way through this world?

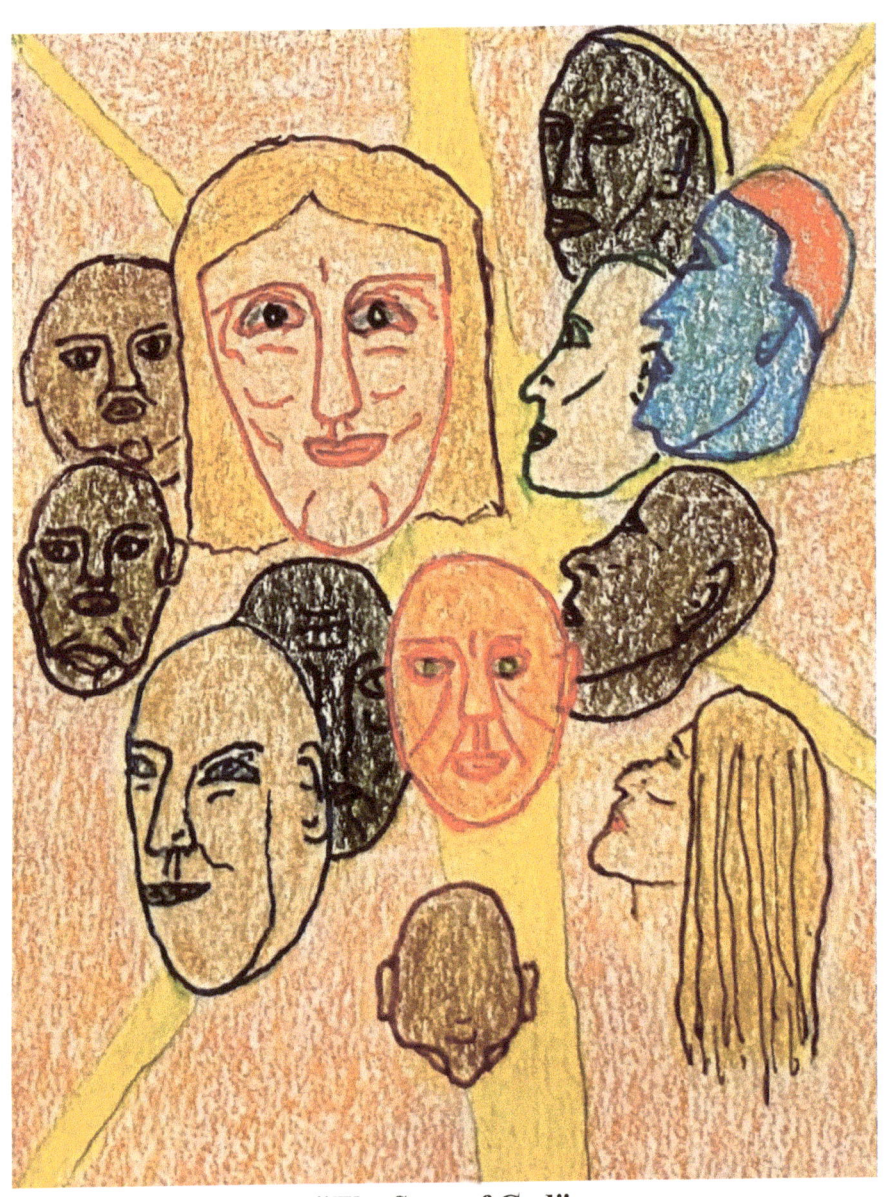

"The Sons of God"
Job 1:6

Mandalas, 26

8. "The Sons of God"

Because the Ultimate One, the Lord, is great and overwhelming, our finite hearts long for beings closer to our size. Such "sons of God" fascinated the ancient world. These were not "sons" in the Christian sense. Humans found (and find!) these would-be godlings attractive for their lesser dimensions.

Such "sons" show up **Job 1:6**: "*There was a certain day, then, when God's sons came so they could present themselves before the Lord. Even Satan was present among them.*"

Yet these "sons of God" do nothing to help as Job suffers through the troubles that follow.

In **Genesis 6:2**,"*God's sons, seeing that* [humanity's] *daughters were beautiful, took them as wives for themselves from all that they picked out.*"

These godlings lust after us for their own good, not ours. What followed in the text were increased wickedness, rebellion, and then a cataclysmic flood.

Those around us may well follow would-be godlings today. God's people do well to remember what scripture teaches, though.

Keep your distance. They aren't your friends

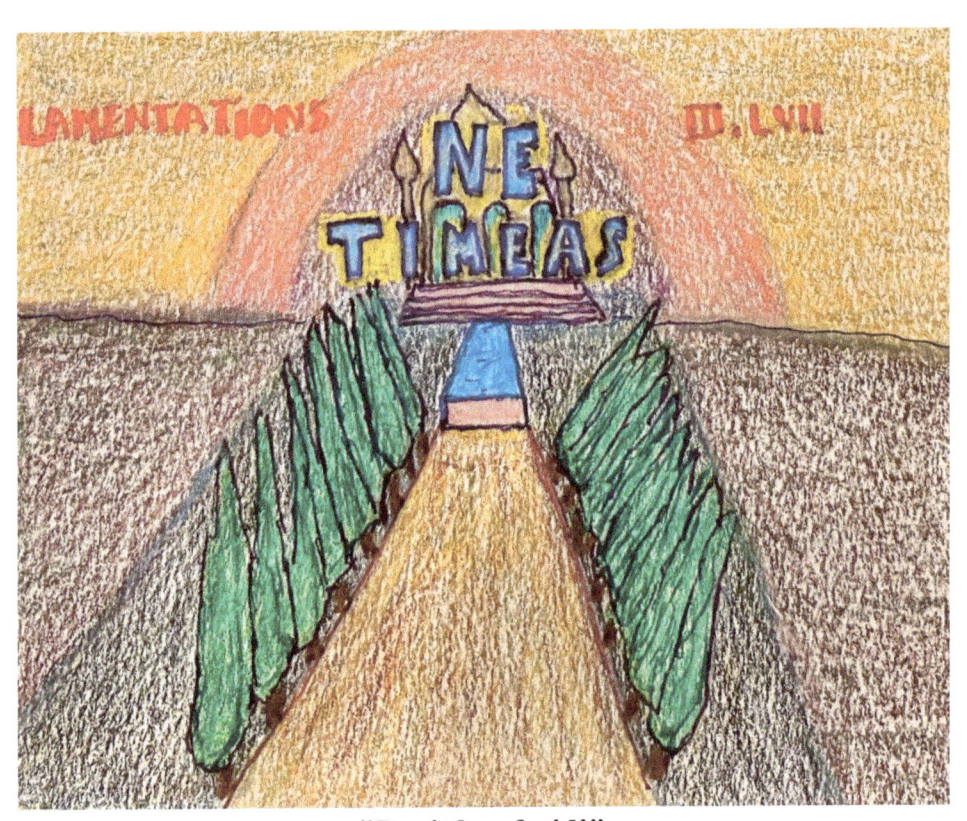

"Don't be afraid!"
Lamentation 3:57

9. "Don't Be Afraid."

Jeremiah the prophet wrote the grievous little Book of Lamentations after the destruction of Jerusalem and the Temple by foreign invaders. The prophet pours out his and his nation's sorrows.

Ancient Israel and its neighbors were Temple states. These were nations built around the worship of their own god in its own place. The surrounding nations fell one by one: Ammonites, Perezzites, Gergashites, Hittites, and others, all inhabitants of the Promised Land before Israel arrived. Those nations did not survive the destruction of their temples.

When the Babylonians destroyed Jerusalem and the Temple, there was no reason to expect a different outcome. This only adds to the intensity of Jeremiah's lament. The Lord is almost entirely silent throughout the work, unlike in Jeremiah's longer prophetic work.

These three words are the only exceptions: "*Don't be afraid*," the Lord says.

The world may be falling apart around you. "*Don't be afraid*."

Your loved ones, your physical body, may be dying. "*Don't be afraid*."

What you believed would guarantee your future may be failing. "*Don't be afraid*."

How can that be so? Jesus' words in **Luke 18:27** come to mind: "*Things that are impossible with men are possible with God*."

The Temple was destroyed. Twenty-six centuries later, God's people endure.

"*Don't be afraid*."

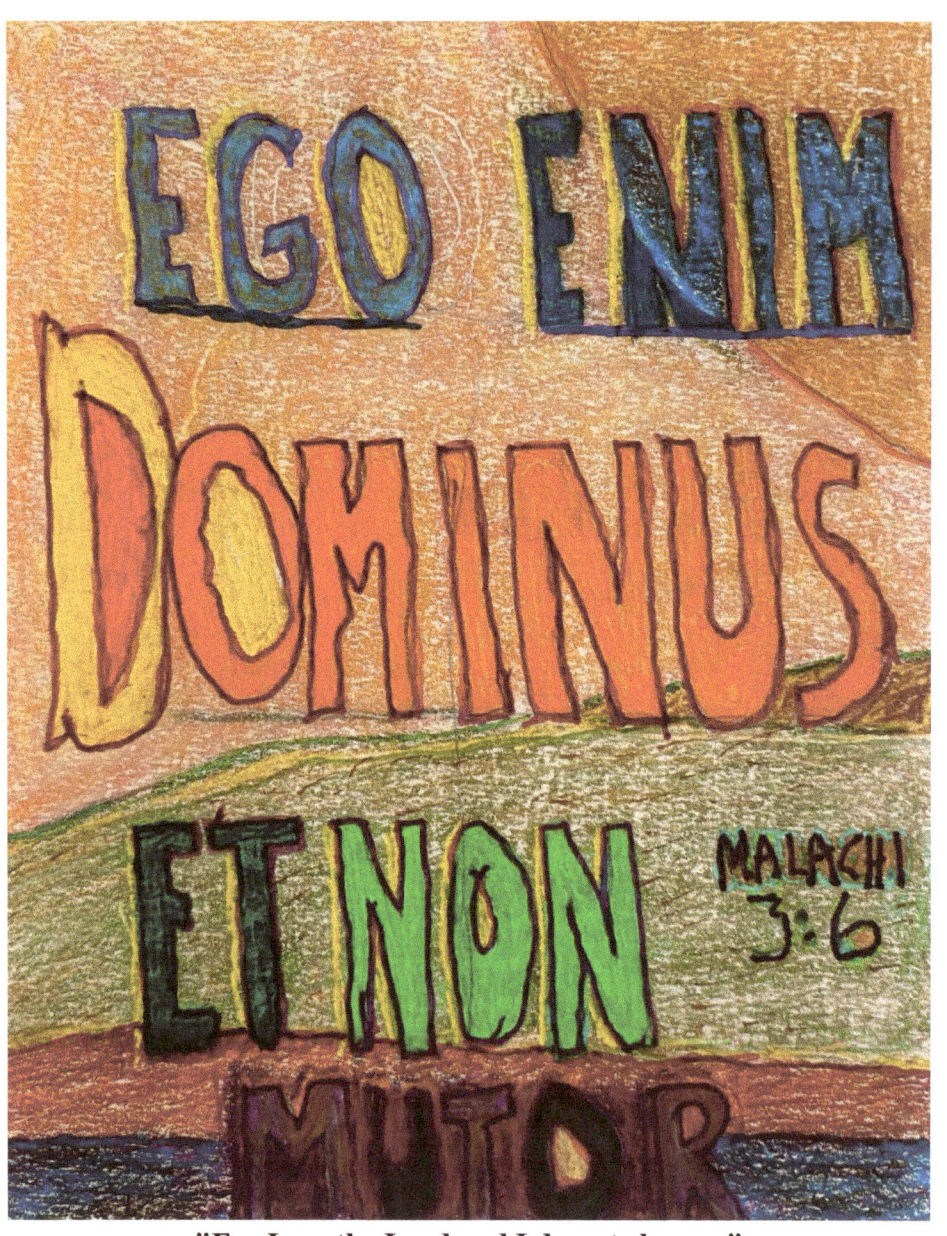

"For I am the Lord and I do not change."
Malachi 3:6

Mandalas, 30

10. "For I Am the Lord and I Do Not Change."

Malachi, author of the last book in the Christian Old Testament, writes after the Temple's destruction, after exile, after the return from exile, and after construction of a less imposing Temple.

The disquiet of the people is obvious in the work. They complain about their reduced circumstances, their ongoing struggles. Through the prophet, the Lord responds by pointing to their reduced faith and ongoing grumbling.

In the midst of this, the Lord tells them in **Malachi 3:6**, "*I am the Lord, and I do not change, and you, Jacob's children, are not consumed.*"

The people's life seems hemmed in by lack, poverty, grumbling, and discontent. There seems to be little spiritual depth or growth. Yet in that very circumstance, this word blazes forth. The Ultimate's unchanging nature is the root of the people's survival.

This is the mystical experience in a sentence. It states in eighteen brief words an insight that the world's sages and seekers sought almost without exception. The Holy One does not change. Because of that, we aren't consumed.

Can we lift our heads out of our aggravation and discontent to accept it?

Mandalas, 31

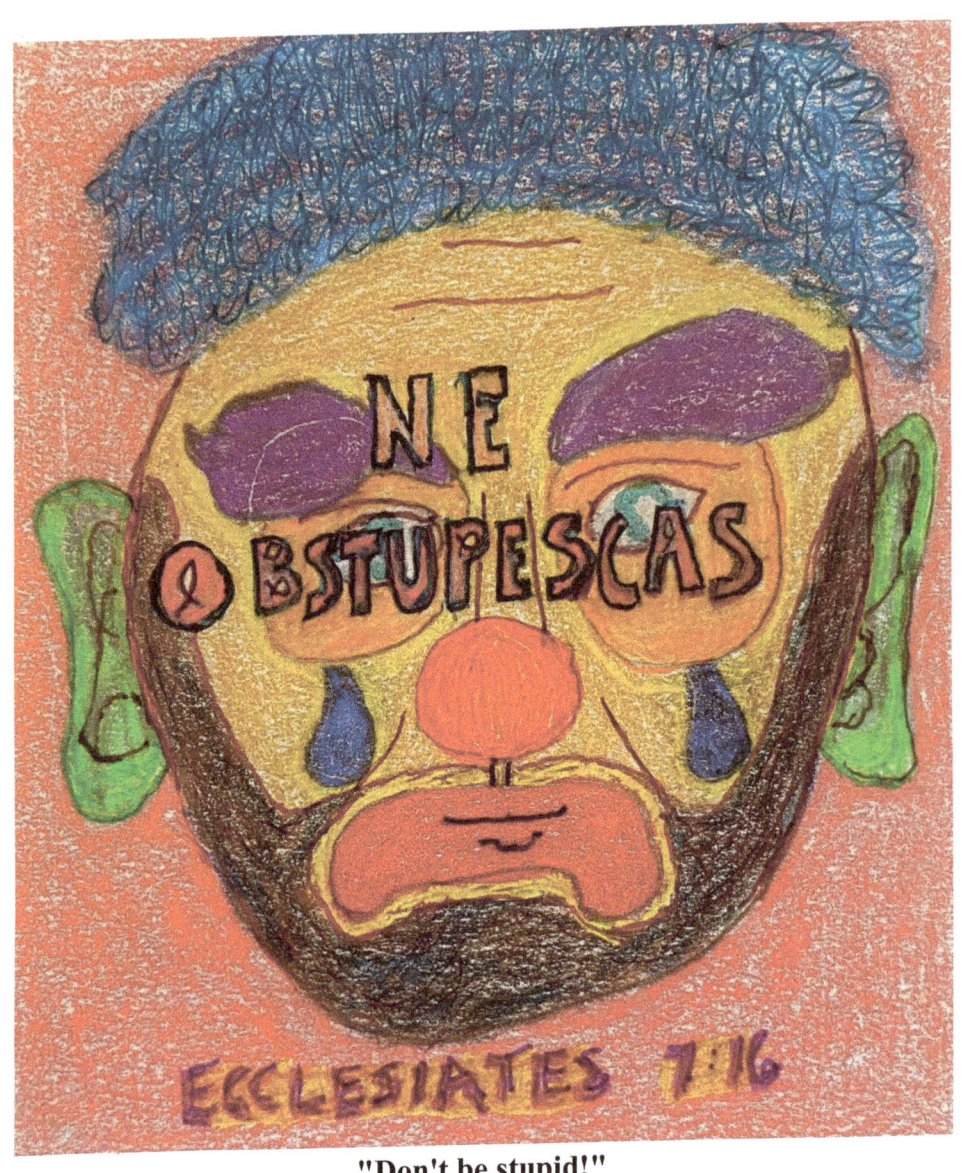

"Don't be stupid!"
Ecclesiastes 7:16

Mandalas, 32

11. "Don't Be Stupid!"

Is this the simplest, most direct guide for ethical living in the Christian Old Testament?

Consider the following quotes from South Asian theologian Vivekananda, quoted from <u>Practical Vedanta</u>:

"Do good if you can, but do not injure the world.

"How can you expect morality to be developed through fear? It can never be.

"Love cannot come through fear, its basis is freedom.

"Truth is nobody's property; no race, no individual can lay any exclusive claim to it. Truth is the nature of all souls.

"He is an atheist who does not believe in himself."

"We all came from God, and we are all bound to go to God, call that God by any name you like; call Him God, or Absolute or Nature, or by any hundred names you like, the fact remains the same. 'From whom all this universe comes out, in whom all that is born lives, and to whom all returns.' This is one fact that is certain."

Or boil it down to what **Ecclesiastes 7:16** says:

"*Don't be stupid.*"

Mandalas, 33

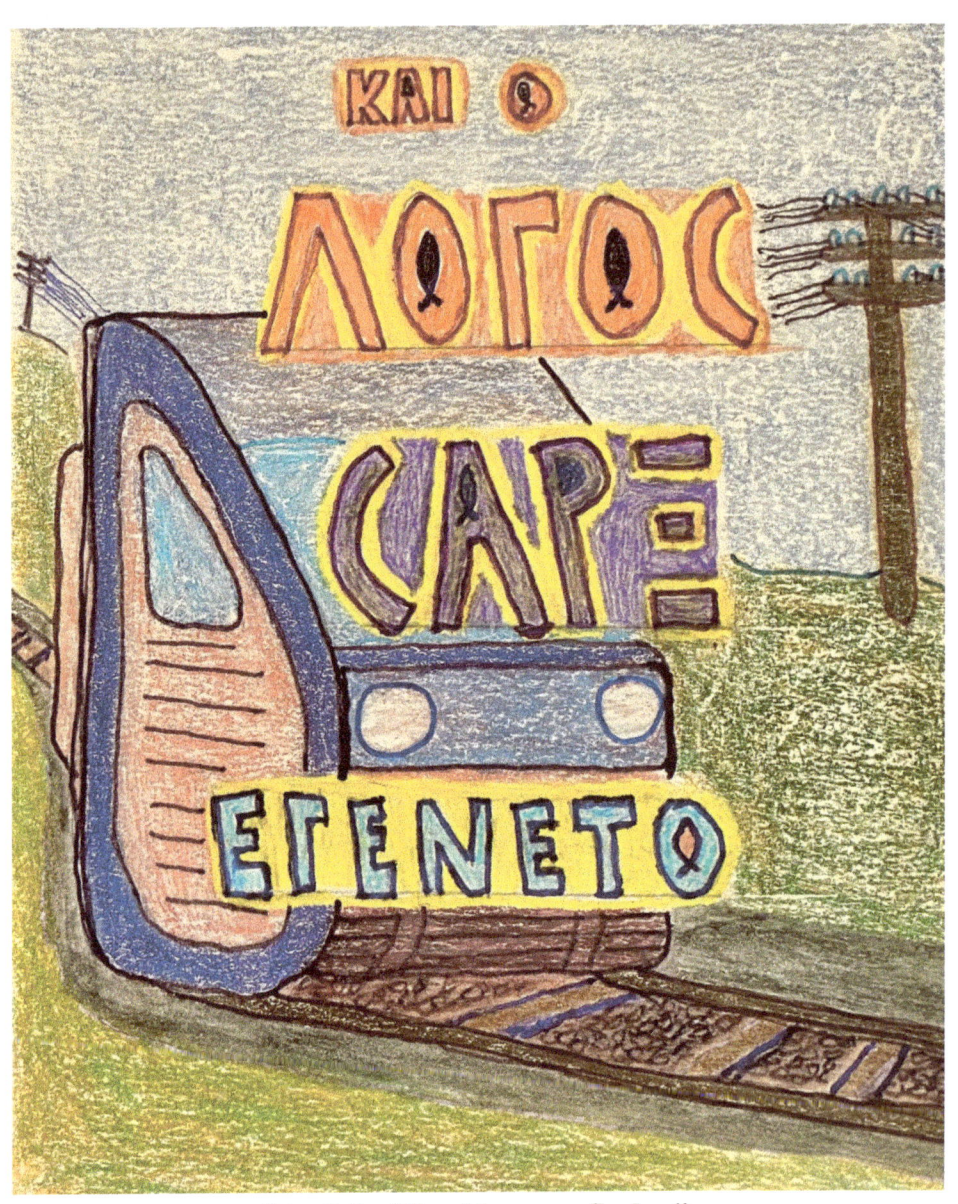

"And the Word became flesh..."
John 1:14

Mandalas, 34

12. "And the Word Became Flesh..."

(Illustrator's Note: many of the oldest Greek inscriptions use a "C" in place of a "Σ". It apparently was dicier to carve a Σ in stone than a C.)

In this passage, John narrates the beginning of the great unveiling of God's nature among us. The Word which spoke the universe into being, the source of "Fiat Lux", enters into human life to the full.

He is no godling, no miniature version of the real thing, unable to help and undermining us by lust. Instead, as **Colossians 1:19** puts it, "*For in him all the fulness of God was pleased to dwell.*"

How can it be that the Ultimate takes flesh in His own creation, among His own creatures? The very idea is repulsive to many among the monotheistic faiths. The act violates the basic principles of ancient philosophers, convinced as they were that the Ultimate cannot change and therefore is not bothered by a world that can.

Yet here He comes. How can this be? We can only answer in the words Jesus spoke to the first two who wondered about it in **John 1:39**: "*Come and see.*"

Mandalas, 35

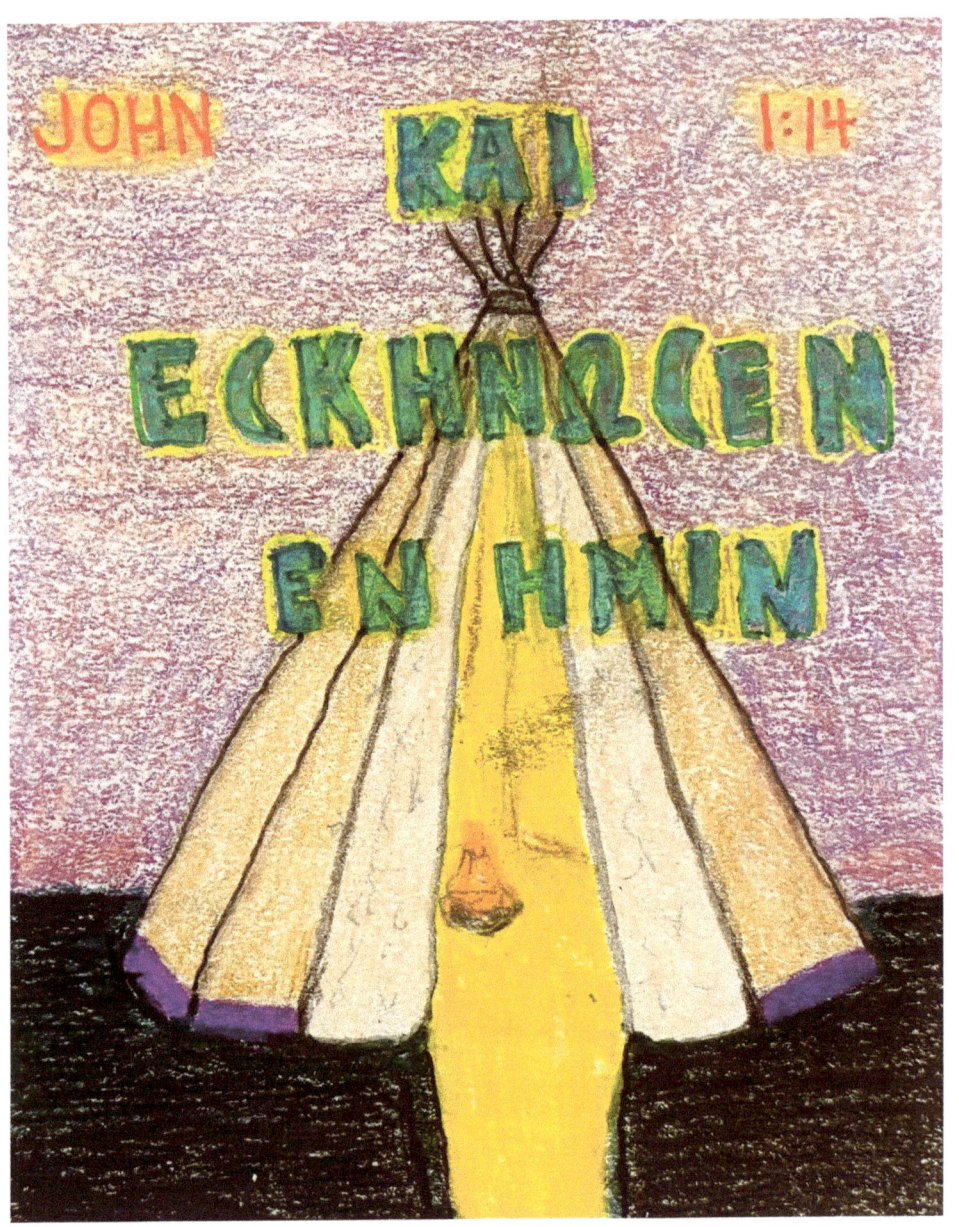

"...and pitched tent among us."
John 1:14

Mandalas, 36

13. "...and Pitched Tent Among Us."

The King James Bible translates this fragment of John **1:14** as "...*and dwelt among us*".

The Greek verb translated as "pitched tent" here, and "dwelt" in the KJV, is formed from the word "*skena*", meaning "tent". The Apostle Paul and his companions in **Acts 18:3** are described as "tentmakers", literally "makers of *skenas*."

In the present day, we've witnessed large populations bombed or driven out of their homes, pitching tents in their own ruined cities just to survive, The Word of God which spoke Creation into being pitches tent among us, in this world to the utmost.

Theologically, Jesus Christ enters into our transient existence in this world of pain, to redeem it.

We, too, find ourselves with our tents pitched here, by a choice others made. Then by our own choices, many of us cause others' tents to be pitched here as well.

As a post script, we derive the English word "scene" from it as well. Backdrops for dramatic performances were painted on "skena", the materials from which tents were made.

The Word of God pitched tent among us. Let that sink in.

Mandalas, 37

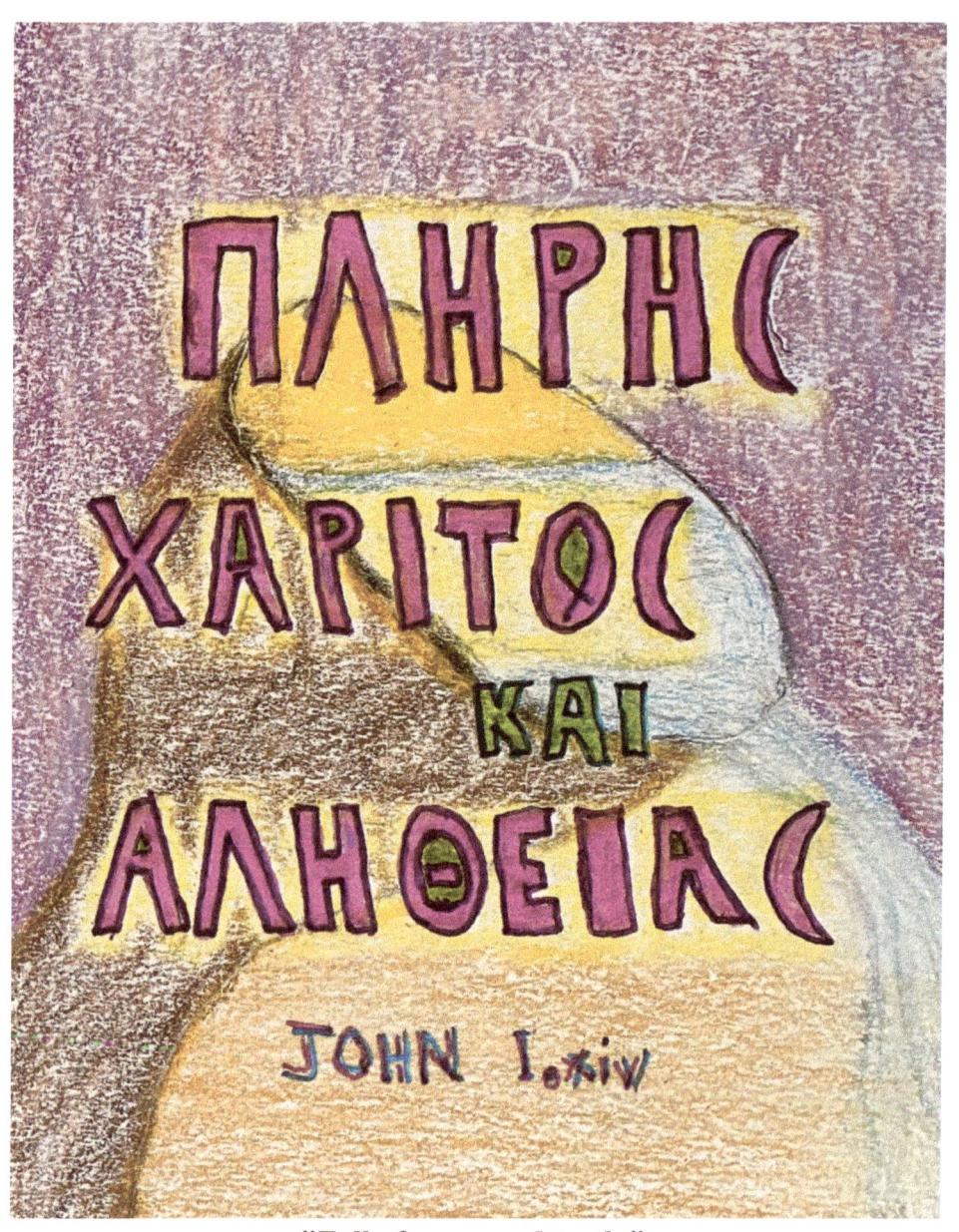

"Full of grace and truth."
John 1:14

Mandalas, 38

14. "...Full of Grace and Truth."

The final fragment of **John 1:14** describes the Word that has "become flesh" and has "pitched tent" among us as "*full of grace and truth.*"

The Ultimate who comes to live among us is not indifferent. He does not deny the reality of this world. He enters it, as said before, to its very depths. And He does so "*full of grace and truth.*"

So many times we stand in need of those same attributes: grace and truth. So often in our world, they are lacking.

But here, in what for Christians is the decisive moment in the story of Creation, "grace and truth" in all their fullness take flesh. Indeed, dynamic grace and truth toward us are among the Ultimate's unchanging properties.

Most of us are full of something. Jesus Christ is full of grace and truth.

What are we full of?

Mandalas, 39

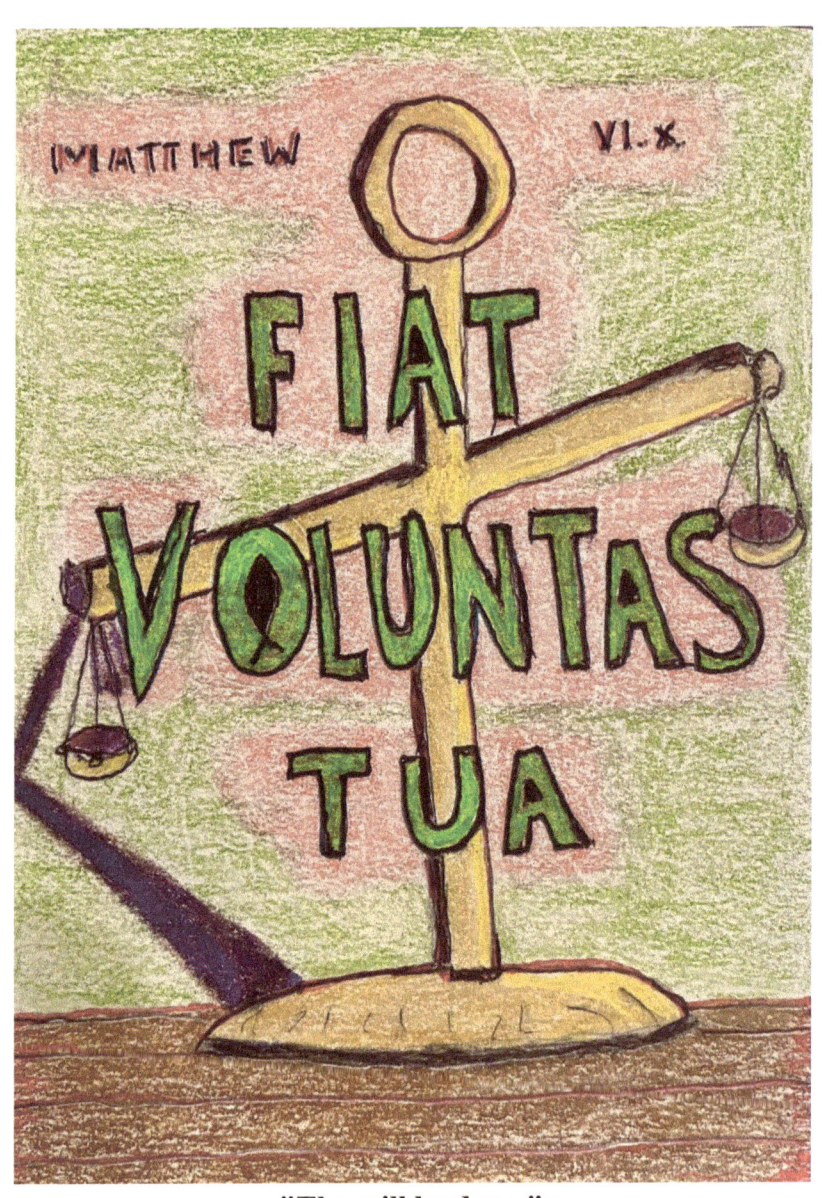

"Thy will be done."
Matthew 6:10

Mandalas, 40

15. Thy Will Be Done.
Matthew 6:10

We find this phrase from the Lord's Prayer in the biblical books of Matthew and in Luke. *"Thy will be done."*

I have a habit of 'praying the scriptures', taking a phrase or verse and repeating it silently with each breath. This phrase is for me among the most challenging to use in such prayer.

Some would say, 'Isn't God's will always done?' What else could it mean to say that God is omnipotent (omni="all"; potent="power")? Ultimately, the laws God establishes will be done, whether we consent to them or not.

But being human means having a measure of free will, at least. In that sphere of human freedom, our obedience to God's will IS a choice. What does it mean, for instance, to *"do justice, love kindness, and walk humbly with our God"*, as **Micah 6:8** enjoins? How about when Jesus commands us to *"Love one another, even as I have loved you,"* in **John 13:34**.

Within that sphere of our relations with ourselves, with each other, with the planet, and with the Lord, do we conform to God's will? The fact that the cycle of life continues without us, the earth rotating on its axis and circling the Sun, is at most times not nearly as relevant as whether we submit our lives to God's expressed will.

Try praying *"Thy will be done."* See what insight those four words shed on your life and action.

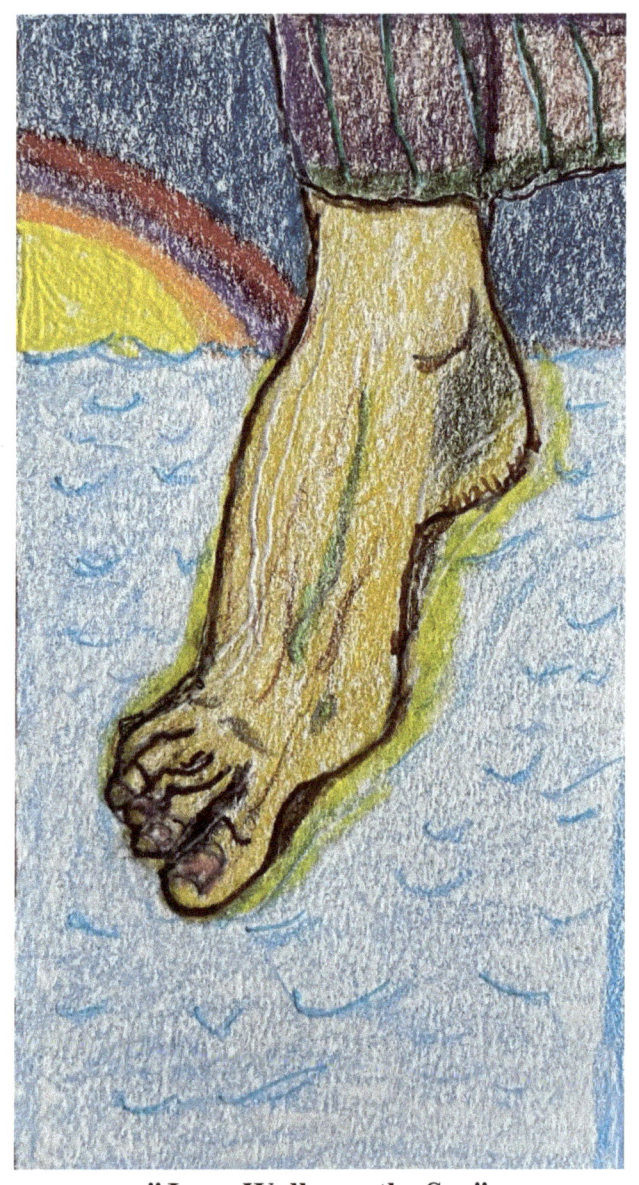

"Jesus Walks on the Sea"
Matthew 14:25-27

Mandalas, 42

16. "Jesus Walks On the Sea."

In **Matthew 14:25-27** we read,

> "[Jesus] *came to them at the night's fourth watch, walking on the sea. They were troubled seeing him walking on the sea, saying that, "It's a ghost!" They shouted for fear. Jesus spoke to them at once, saying, "Have faith! I am. Don't be afraid!"*

Of course, our first response is disbelief, just as it was for the disciples. This stuff can't happen, we say. In fact, say others, these alleged miracles are why so many turn away.

I encourage you to at least suspend disbelief for a moment or two. What would it mean in your life that the Ultimate walks upon the storms and chaos of life? He doesn't do it just because He can. He does it **to seek us in our hours of struggle, as He sought the disciples long ago**

Also, notice the foot taking the step. It is not pedicured and polished. It is, instead, battered and bruised. Yet despite the foot's condition, the One whose foot it is treads the storm in pursuit of frightened seekers overwhelmed by the elements.

Such is the foot of the One seeking us.

What does it mean for us that this is true?

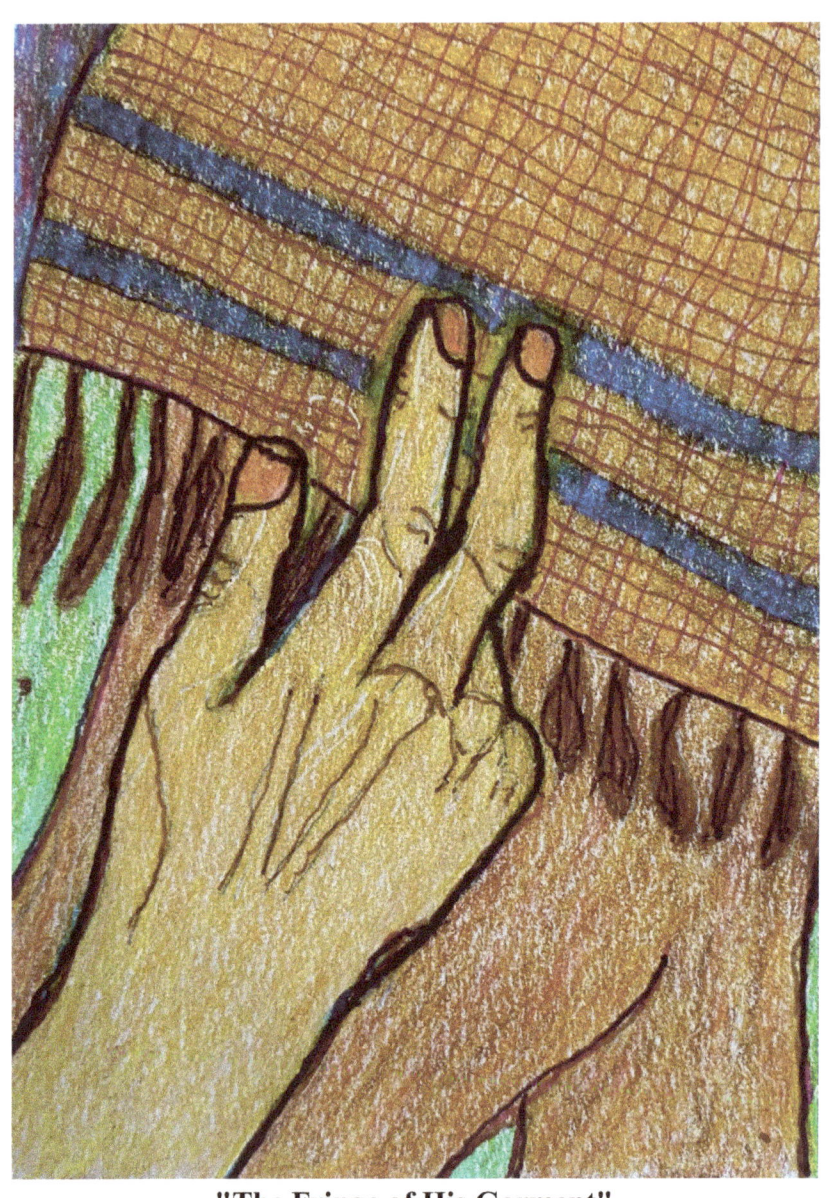

"The Fringe of His Garment"
Mark 6:56

Mandalas, 44

17. "The Fringe of His Garment."

Mark 6:56

"*Wherever* [Jesus] *entered, in towns or in villages or in cities, they put the sick in the streets and begged him that they might touch the fringe of his clothing – and as many as touched him were made whole.*"

In **Mark 5:21-35**, a woman who had suffered a flow of blood for twelve years came up behind Jesus in a crowd, touched the fringe of His garment, and was healed.

In **Numbers 15:38-41**, the Lord commanded Israel's men to wear such fringes as an ongoing reminder of His presence and Law.

Zechariah 8:23 prophesied the day when, "*...they will grab the garment's fringe of a Jewish man, saying, 'We will go with you, for we have heard that God is with you.'*"

In the South Asian tradition, *Chandogya Upanishad* says, "There is a bridge between time and eternity; and this bridge is Atman, the Spirit of man... Evil or sin cannot cross that bridge, because the world of the Spirit is pure. This is why when this bridge has been crossed, the eyes of the blind can see, the wounds of the wounded are healed, and the sick man becomes whole from his sickness. To one who goes over that bridge, the night becomes like day; because in the worlds of the Spirit there is a light which is everlasting."

Jesus embodies the "bridge between time and eternity." His garment's fringe represents "*...that God is with you.*"

Imagine in the depths of your soul approaching Him and touching the fringe of His garment.

Mandalas, 45

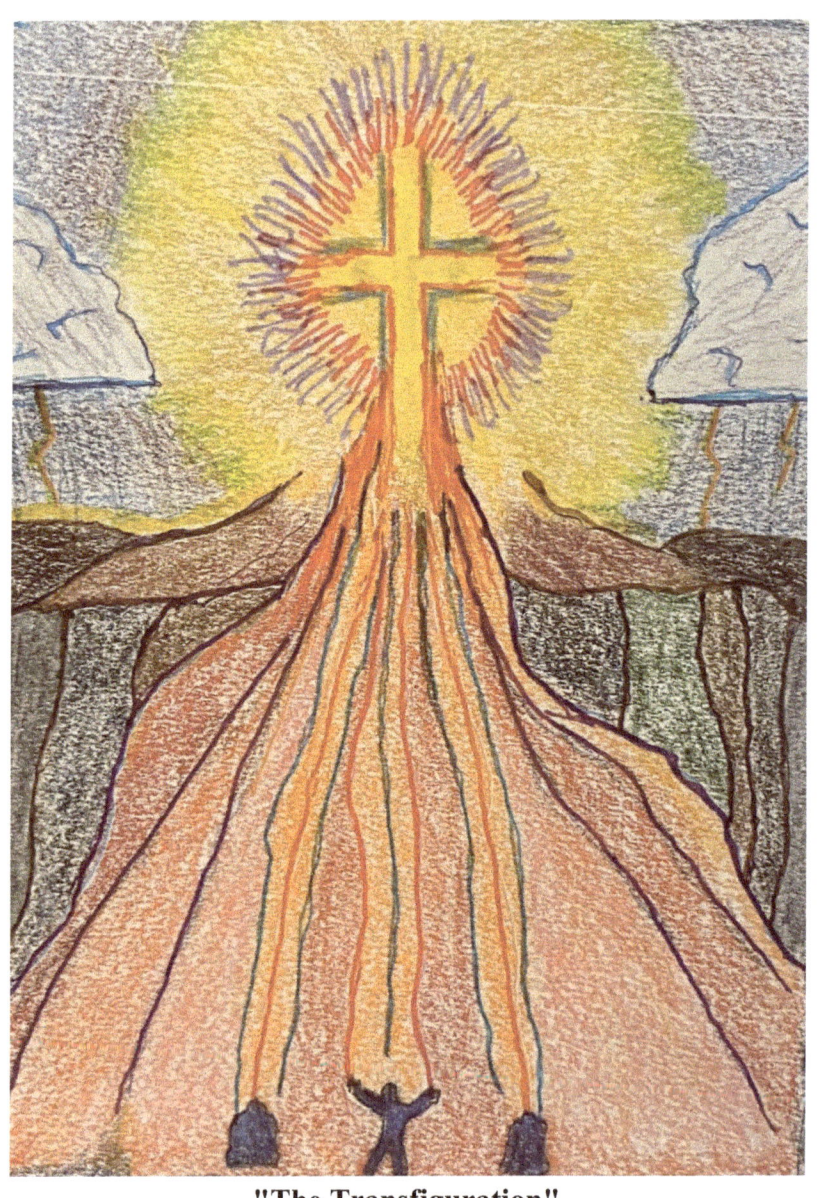

"The Transfiguration"
Luke 9:28-36

Mandalas, 46

18. "The Transfiguration."

There comes a moment in our walk with Jesus when He is transfigured before us. In that moment, the veneer of mere mortality fades, and His identity as the Ultimate in flesh shines through.

For Peter, James, and John, that moment happened on the Mount of Transfiguration, as they followed Jesus to Jerusalem. **Luke 9:28-29** puts it this way:
> "*Around eight days after these words, he took Peter and John and James and climbed up onto a mountain so he could pray. While he prayed, his face's appearance changed, and his clothing was shining white.*"

On one level, Jesus doesn't seem to be doing anything extraordinary. He's just praying, something that he often did.

Yet in the midst of that 'ordinary', of Jesus being Jesus, the veil is drawn back and His disciples see Him as He is. They see visions of saints from heaven. They hear the Voice of the Infinite One.

Of course, they are terrified. Yet Jesus calms their fears, and they continue on.

The key fact to remember is that Peter, James, and John persisted in following Jesus, before and after. Had they given up before, they would never have seen Him transfigured. Had they given up after, they would never have found the courage to face what lay ahead.

But they did follow. They did see. They did find courage, not from themselves but from the Lord.

I pray it may be so for us!

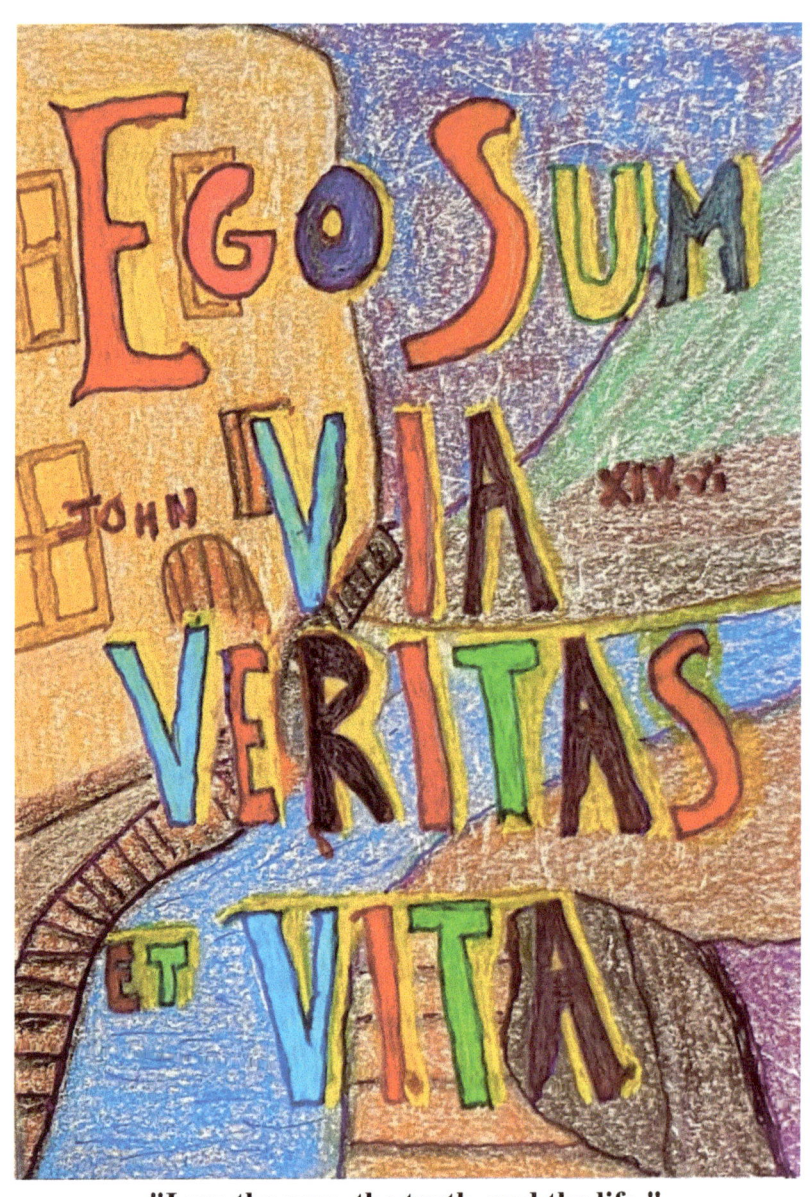

"I am the way, the truth, and the life."
John 14:6

Mandalas, 48

19. "I Am the Way, the Truth, and the Life."

John 14:5-6

"Thomas says to him, 'Lord, we don't know where you are going, and how can we know the way?' Jesus says to him, 'I am the way and the truth and the life. No one comes to the Father except through me.'"

Theologians, mystics, and philosophers argue long over the nature of the Ultimate. Is it the "God of the philosophers"? Is it an impersonal Absolute, including both what we know as 'God' and what we call 'Creation'? Is it incomprehensible Brahman?

Jesus answers with a boldness that seems foolish under the circumstances: in a room with a dozen disciples, knowing that betrayal, arrest, trial, torture and death were but a few hours a way.

"I am the way," he claims, *"the truth, and the life."*

How can that be? Is He not just a human like the rest of us? The events of the following hours will answer. Yes, He is human, just like us. He is subject to sorrow, physical pain, bodily injury, and death. All that will be amply demonstrated.

Yet when He rises on Sunday morning, He reveals He is also the human face of the Ultimate. This Ultimate is not isolated, unmoved, uncaring. He is alongside, seeking, redeeming. The Ultimate is not changed by anything outside, yet changes Himself out of dynamic love and redeeming grace.

This sentence can be read as evangelical imperialism. One either knows Him as we do or one has no hope. Yet it can also be read as saying wherever human lives are touched by the Ultimate, wherever they are transformed, wherever the marks of divine love are manifest, there is Christ.

Way, truth, and life! What wondrous markers for the Ultimate made known!

Mandalas, 49

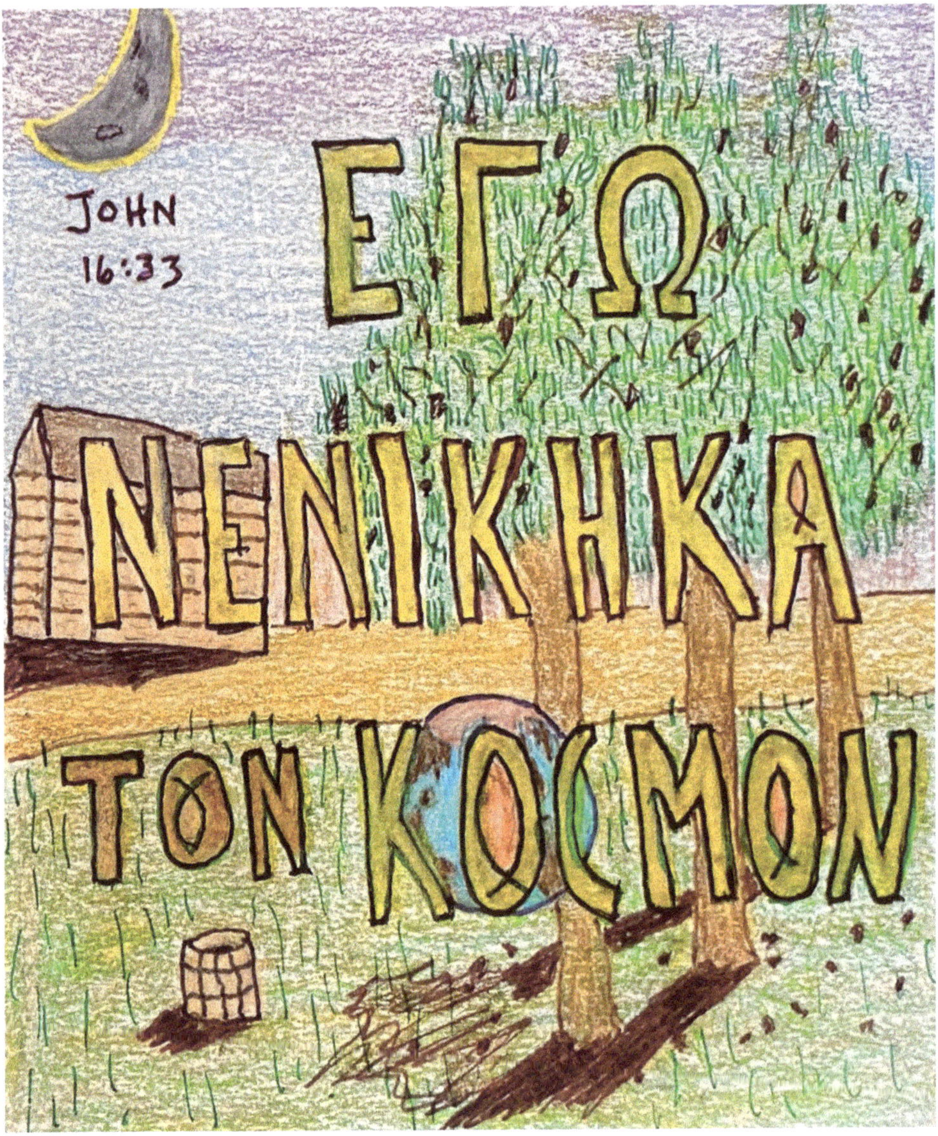
ΕΓΩ
ΝΕΝΙΚΗΚΑ
ΤΟΝ ΚΟϹΜΟΝ
JOHN
16:33

Mandalas, 50

20. "I Have Overcome the World."

My Biblical and theological training taught me that context is crucial in understanding scripture. Verses out of context can be twisted to make them say pretty much what the speaker wants them to say.

Consider the context of this text. It was not spoken at a moment of triumph. Jesus had not just finished destroying His enemies or establishing His earthly kingdom.

He spoke these words, like those in the previous mandala, in an upper room, with a dozen or so disciples. He spoke them, according to the text, knowing full well what awaited Him in just a few hours: betrayal, arrest, condemnation, torture, and death.

We would no doubt say, 'What irony to have spoken so in such circumstances'. How foolish we might feel, as yet another failed dreamer's words fizzle.

Yet the story following these words leads not just to immense suffering and sorrow. It leads to Resurrection.

As I prayed this verse recently, it struck me to hear the Speaker here as the deepest Source of life, including my own life. "**I got this,**" He says.

The verb is past perfect tense: an action fully completed already. The Greek word for victory, "*Nike*", peeks out in the middle of it. (It's also the name of a shoe brand of some sort.)

Wherever we are, whatever our circumstance, hear life's Ultimate reality speak these words to us and for us:

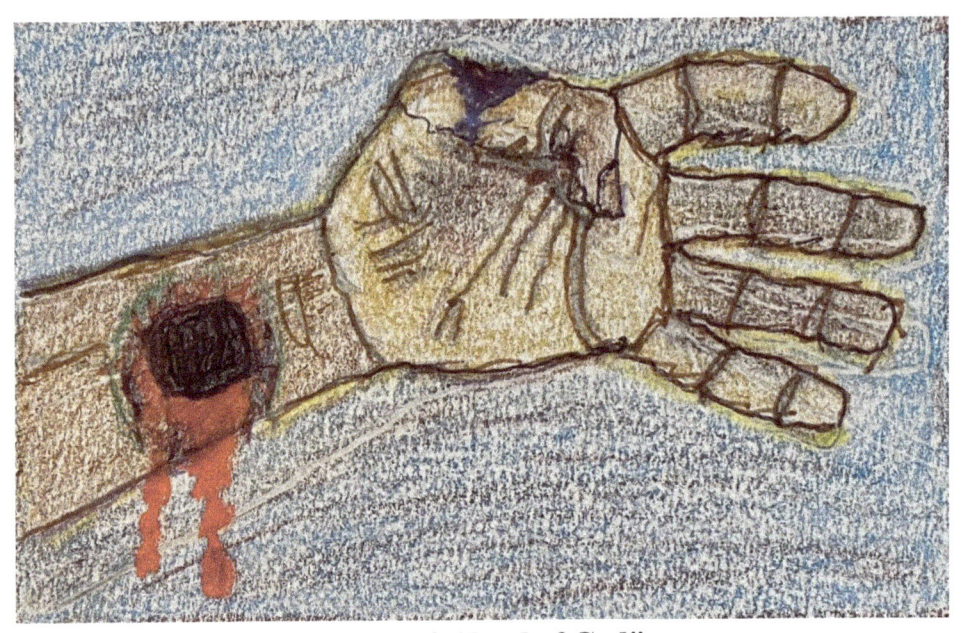

"The Left Hand of God"

"I have overcome the world."

21. "The Left Hand of God."

God's triumph in our midst is not that of the indestructible. Christ does not live among us with an exemption from the pain all of us face. Redeeming us from sin, death, and futility bears a grievous cost.

Sometimes we are tempted to feel abandoned in this life's hardship. We wonder with Job what we ever did to deserve this.

On the other hand, when things break our way in life we are tempted to take all the credit for ourselves. Aren't we wonderful, we think. Of course we deserve this!

All our lives, the good and the bad, are redeemed under the shadow of the left hand of God. God's right hand reaches out to us in Jesus Christ, as it were, winning us to Himself and to the peace which He intends as our destiny.

Yet the left hand bears the marks of the price He paid to open that way before us.

This is no impersonal Absolute, no indifferent Ultimate.

It is a loving Father, who forever bears the scars of our redemption.

Mandalas, 53

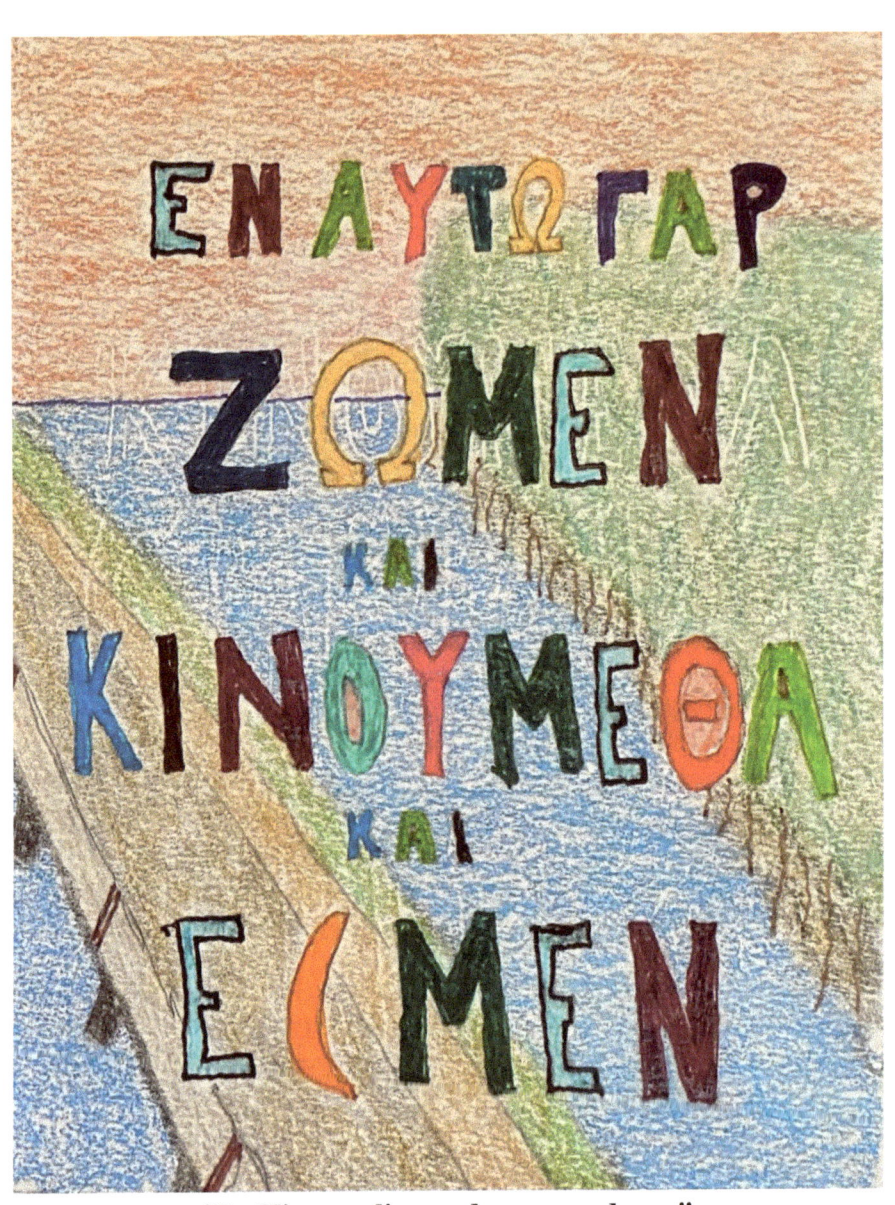

"In Him, we live and move and are."
Acts 17:28

Mandalas, 54

22. "In Him, We Live, and Move, and Are."
Acts 17:28

This verse in the Revised Standard Version reads, "*In him we live and move and have our being.*" The original Greek is more direct, as reflected in the translation here.

This verse is the first Christian reference to a non-Judeo-Christian source. The Apostle Paul quotes the Greek poet Epimenides, as he preaches in Athens in the Book of Acts.

Epimenides, in turn, expressed an insight shared by his South Asian contemporaries.

It remains true today. We live, move, and are in Him.

Let that anchor your heart today.

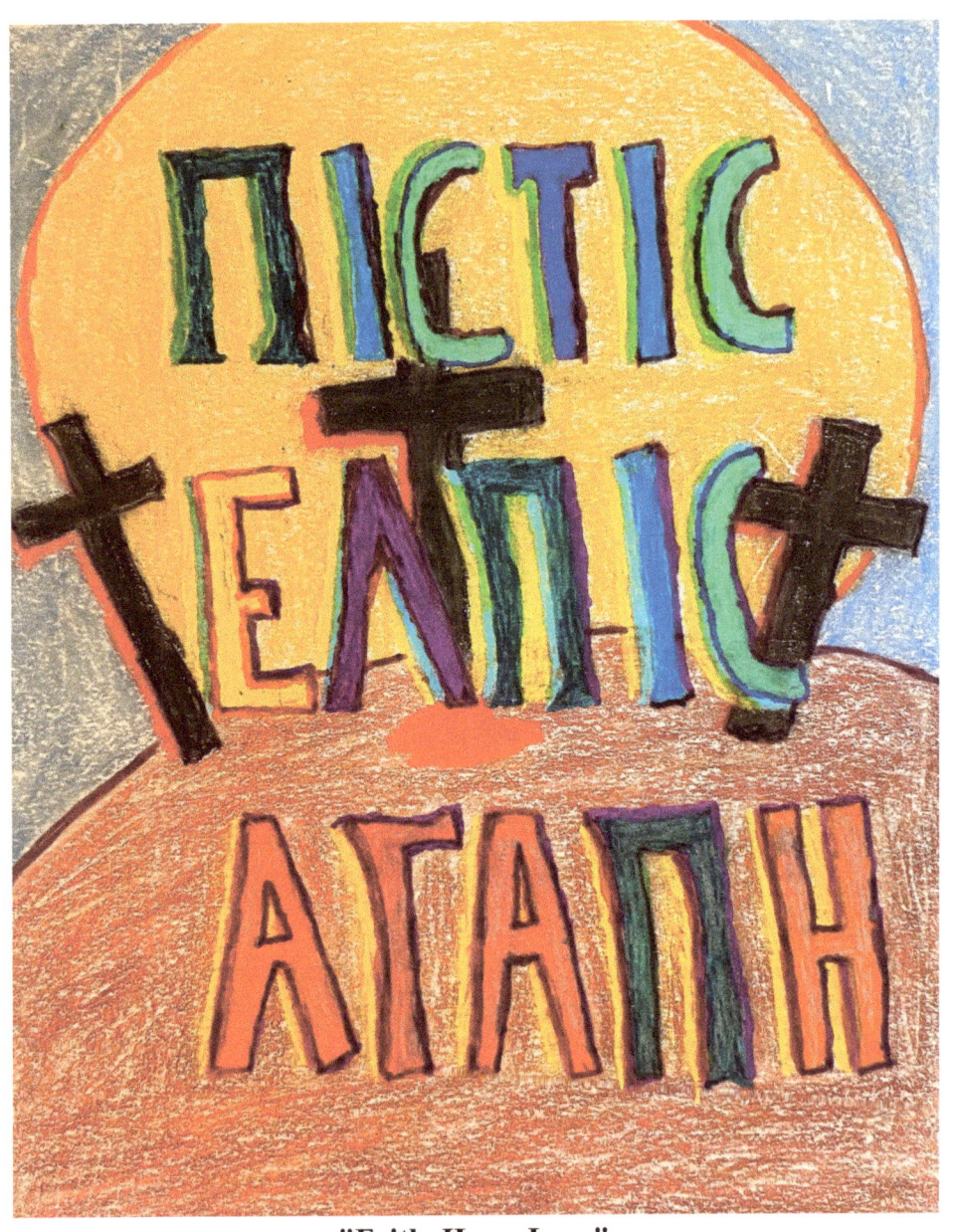

"Faith, Hope, Love"
1 Corinthians 13:13

Mandalas, 56

23. "Faith, Hope, Love."

Paul the Apostle writes at the end of the famous "Love Chapter" in **1 Corinthians 13:13**, "*But now faith, hope, love abide, these three – but the greatest of these is love.*"

Paul himself knew the suffering that accompanied life in Christ in this world. Both the Book of Acts and his own New Testament letters bear witness to the man's suffering on behalf of his faith.

To this day, he is reviled as often as any other character in scripture. We question his motives, condemn his assumptions, reject his intentions.

Yet his witness remains, even when misunderstood, even when distorted.

Ask yourself what abides, what endures, in our spiritual lives.

May it come to be "*faith, hope, and love*" as well!

Mandalas, 57

"For freedom Christ has set us free."
Galatians 5:1

Mandalas, 58

24. "For Freedom Christ Has Set Us Free."

"For freedom Christ has set us free."
Galatians 5:1

As stated elsewhere in this work, freedom in Christ is not simply license to do whatever we want, whenever we want it. According to the Gospel, the Ultimate itself has entered into human life, willingly submitted to the bonds of our fleshly life, to bring us into intimate relation with itself.

When we identify ourselves with the passions, desires, or objects of this earth, we lose that freedom. Our fate intertwines with the fates of those things which captivate us. When they change, crumble, come to an end, we feel the weight of those chains bearing down on us to our misery.

Yet Christ has freed us, so that we no longer need to be bound by these things. As fragile human beings, we are liable to the pain and losses of the world. As participants in the Body of Christ, though, we are beyond harm and loss. It depends on how we orient ourselves: to this earthly life, or to the Ultimate Christ.

Orienting ourselves to Christ does not mean abandoning our role in life. It need not make us passive. It does mean we are free to engage in the world without the gripping fear that if we fail in a worldly sense, our lives fail as well.

Christ set us free so we may live as free women and men, here and now and forever.

Do you live your freedom?

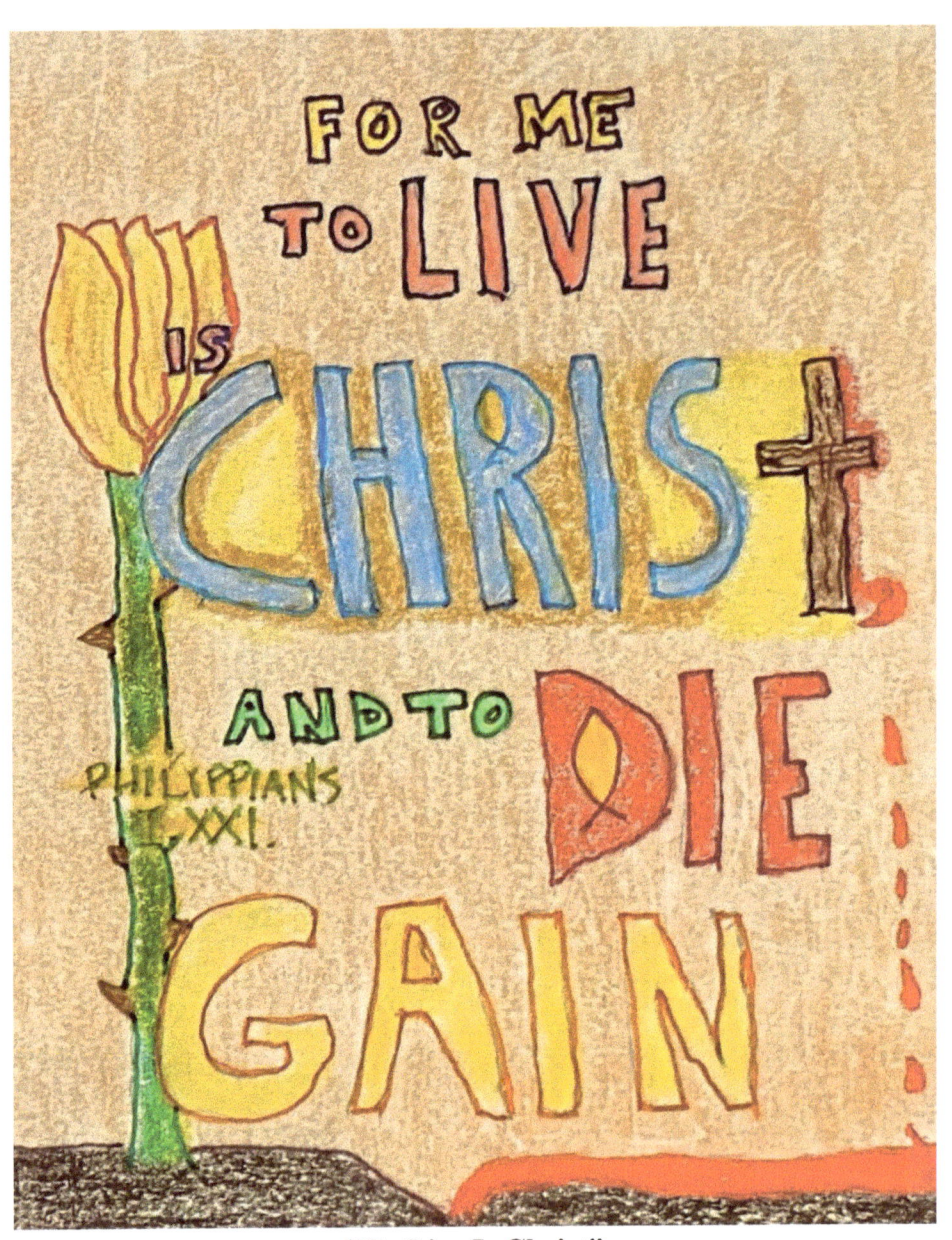

"To Live Is Christ"
Philippians 1:21

Mandalas, 60

25. "To Live Is Christ."

"For me, to live is Christ, and to die gain."
Philippians 1:21

Once again, we see the importance of context to understanding scripture. It would be one thing to write the words quoted above in a comfortable old age, surrounded by loved ones and with physical needs secured. Paul's situation when he wrote was something else entirely.

Paul wrote this most gentle of his epistles from prison. He had suffered greatly in the course of his ministry: beatings, imprisonments, failed executions, even a shipwreck. Those of us who stress out about the small things in life probably would view his situation as a complete disaster.

Yet Paul is untroubled by it from an earthly standpoint. He tells the Philippians he is torn between wanting to go (die) and be with the Lord or stay (live) and continue his work. At that point, he writes, *"For me, to live is Christ and to die gain."*

What manner of prayer and practice would we need to come to a similar point? This is not an attitude that disdains this life, but that lives here knowing its completion is elsewhere, in Christ, forever.

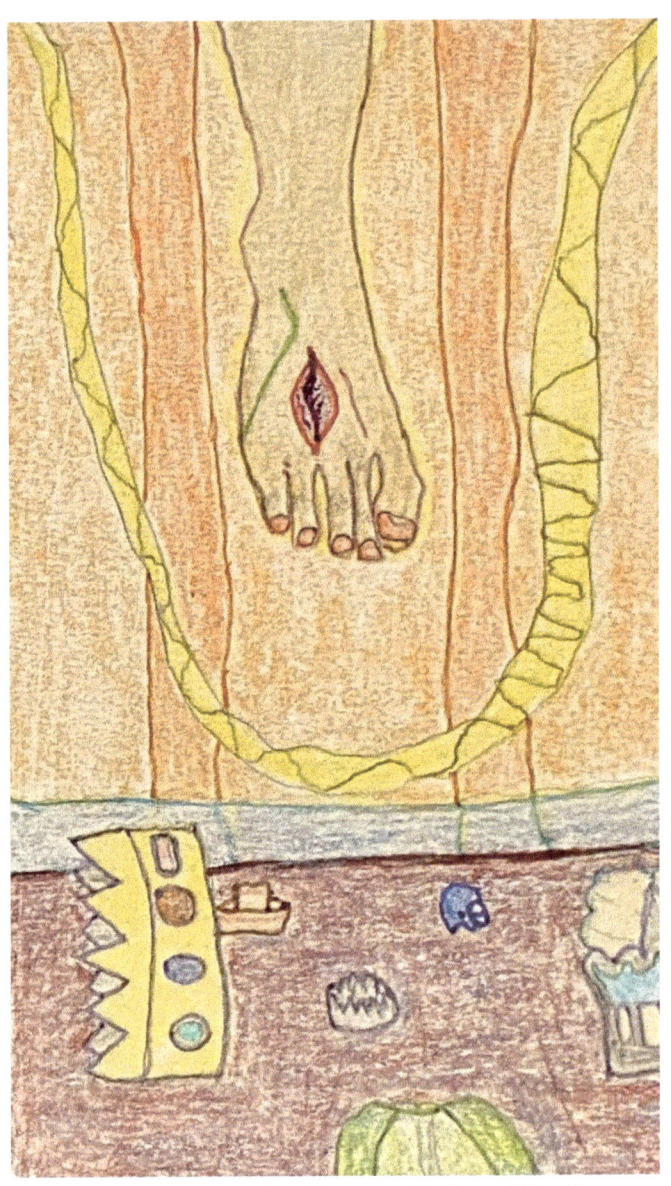

"Casting Their Crowns Before Him"
Revelation 4:10

Mandalas, 62

26. "Casting Their Crowns Before Him."

"...the twenty-four elders will fall down before the One sitting on the throne, and will worship the One living in ages of ages, and will cast their crowns before the throne."
Revelation 4:10

When we are young, this world seems to offer many rewards. We work (or maybe just long for without working!) the world's honors, riches, and power. We envy those who have more of those things than us, and look down on those with less. Somehow, however many honors we win, however many riches we pile up, however much power we accumulate, it isn't enough.

Katha Upanishad teaches us, "The Creator made the senses outward-going: they go to the world of matter outside, not to the Spirit within... The foolish run after outward pleasures and fall into the snares of vast-embracing death."

In the Book of Revelation, however, we are given a different vision. There, twenty-four elders who have gained all this world has to offer gladly cast down those crowns before the glory of the Lord. Nothing we can gain (or lose!) in this world amounts to even a fraction of the blessing of God's presence.

Surrender it all before Him! Cast down those crowns this world holds so dear! What blazes up before you is so immensely more rewarding.

Mandalas, 63

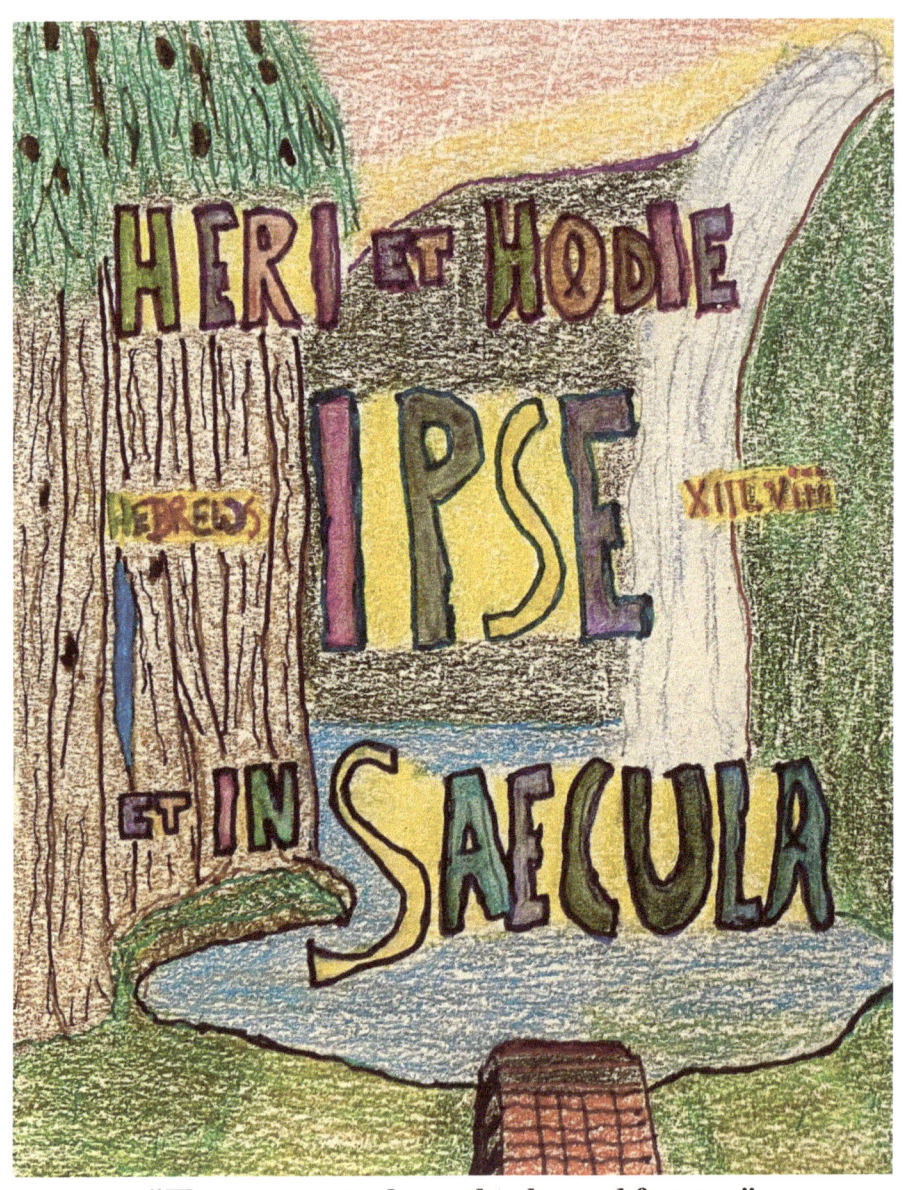

"The same yesterday and today and forever."
Hebrews 13:8

Mandalas, 64

27. "The Same Yesterday and Today and Forever."

The writer of the Letter of Hebrews says in **Hebrews 13:8**, "*Jesus Christ is the same yesterday, and today, and forever.*"

Hebrew, Greek, Christian, Muslim, and South Asian theologians all came to a measure of agreement on the unchanging nature of that Ultimate we call God.

As I've emphasized before, one aspect of that unchanging Ultimate is its dynamic love and grace toward those who suffer and seek. The philosophers sometimes struggle to accept this. The sufferers, on the other hand, receive it with profound gratitude and relief.

The Christian revelation agrees that the Abyss of the Father, as St. Gregory of Nazianzus called it, is utterly beyond our ability to grasp. Unaided, we might have an inkling of its existence, but all else would simply be our projections upon it.

Yet we are not unaided. The Ultimate who is "*the same yesterday and today and forever*" has a name, a name it has chosen to reveal to us. It has a character, revealed also in the One whose name we've been told.

Jesus Christ, who loved us and gave His life to bring us to the Father, "*is the same yesterday and today and forever.*"

I know no greater comfort.

Mandalas, 65

Mandalas, 66

South Asian Traditions

Mandalas, 67

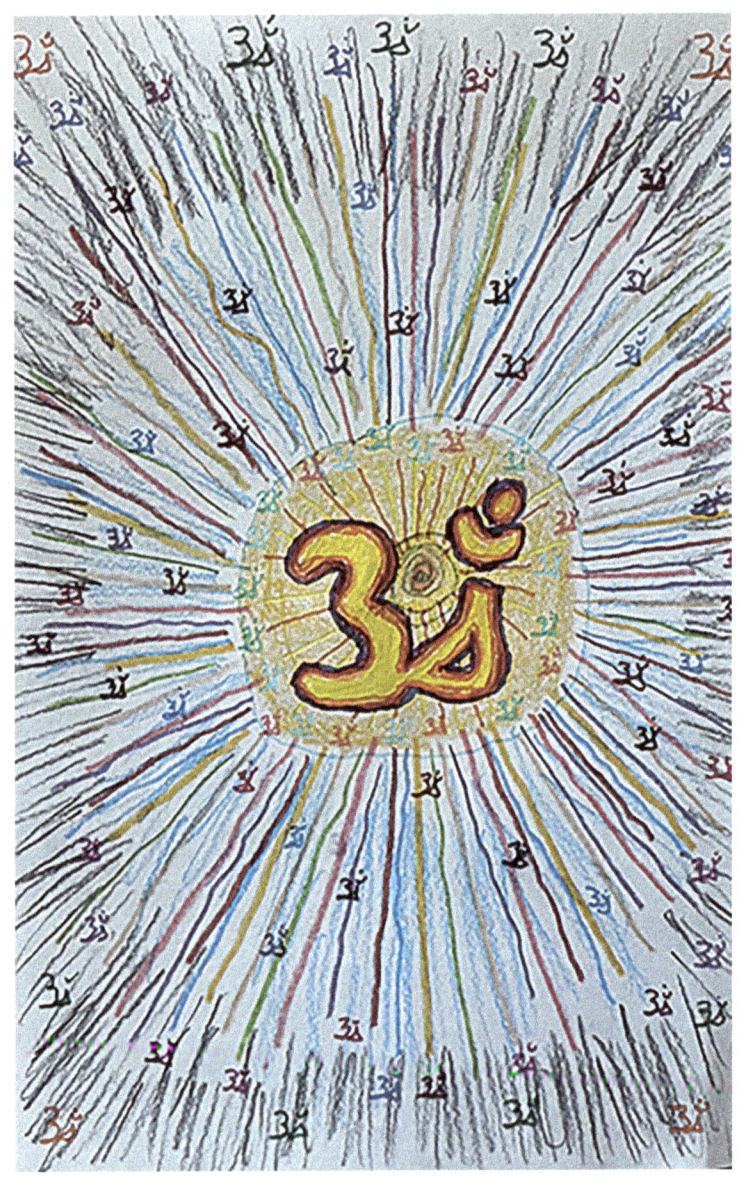

"Aum Universal"

Mandalas, 68

28. "Aum Universal."

I have been wary of publicly using this symbol, associated as it is with the religious traditions of South Asia. I know many of my evangelical Christian friends look upon it with suspicion, if not hostility. The symbol itself, though, predates present day Hinduism and Buddhism.

It is pronounced as "awm", like the English word "awe" with a closing "m". The word comes from Sanskrit, a language pre-dating the invention of writing. Sanskrit shares a common root with so-called Indo-European languages, among them Greek, Latin, German, French, Spanish, and English.

The alphabet used is called *Devanagari*. Ancient South Asian writers used *Devanagari* to put the spoken language of Sanskrit into a written form.

Aum, as I spell it here, is the Ultimate. South Asian schools considered the literal sound of the word itself a connection to the Ultimate. Saying it aloud or in one's thoughts was considered prayer. It entered into their scriptures and worship in the distant past.

Some speculate that the aboriginal common tongue which gave us the spoken word Aum predates the separation between the Indo-European and the Semitic language families. Semitic languages include Hebrew, Aramaic, and Arabic, among others. In this view, Aum continues into these languages as Amen in Hebrew and Ameen in Arabic. I lack the linguistic chops to do say whether or not that is true.

Nevertheless, on the tongues of vast numbers of humans through the millennia, Aum has been the primal word from which the universe emerges.

It is at least similar to the idea expressed in **John 1:1** and **1:14** in the Christian Bible: "*In the beginning the Word was, and the Word was with God, and the Word was God*", and "*The Word became flesh, and lived among us, and we saw His glory, glory like the only-born from the Father, full of grace and truth.*"

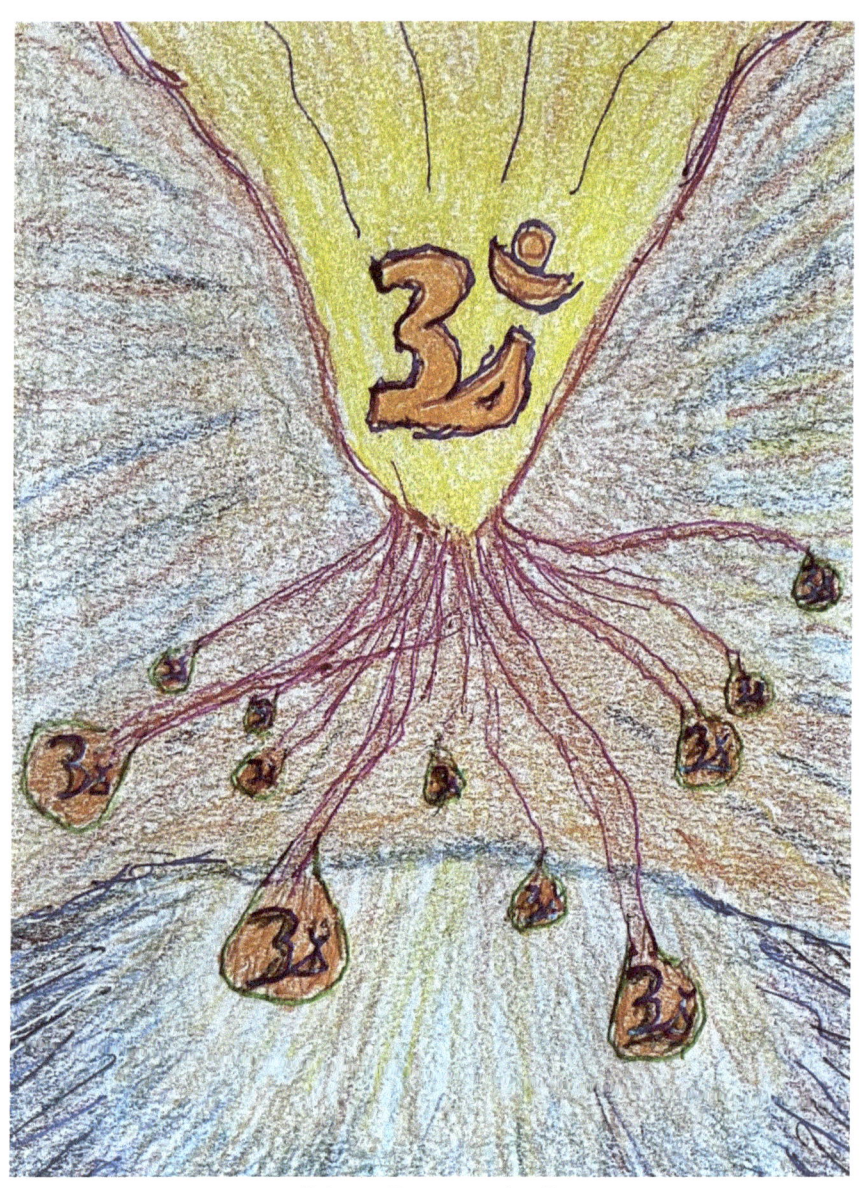

"Aum Penetrative"

Mandalas, 70

29. "Aum Penetrative."

This mandala represents the fact that the same Aum manifests in every created life. *Brihad-Aranyaka Upanishad* teaches us the following:

"The source of all names is the word, for it is by the word that all names are spoken. The word is behind all names, even as Brahman is behind the word.

"The immortal is veiled by the real. The Spirit of life is the immortal. Name and form are the real, and by them the Spirit is veiled."

"Maitreyi [an ancient sage] said, 'What should I do then with possessions that cannot give me life eternal? Give me instead your knowledge, o my lord.'"

Mandalas, 71

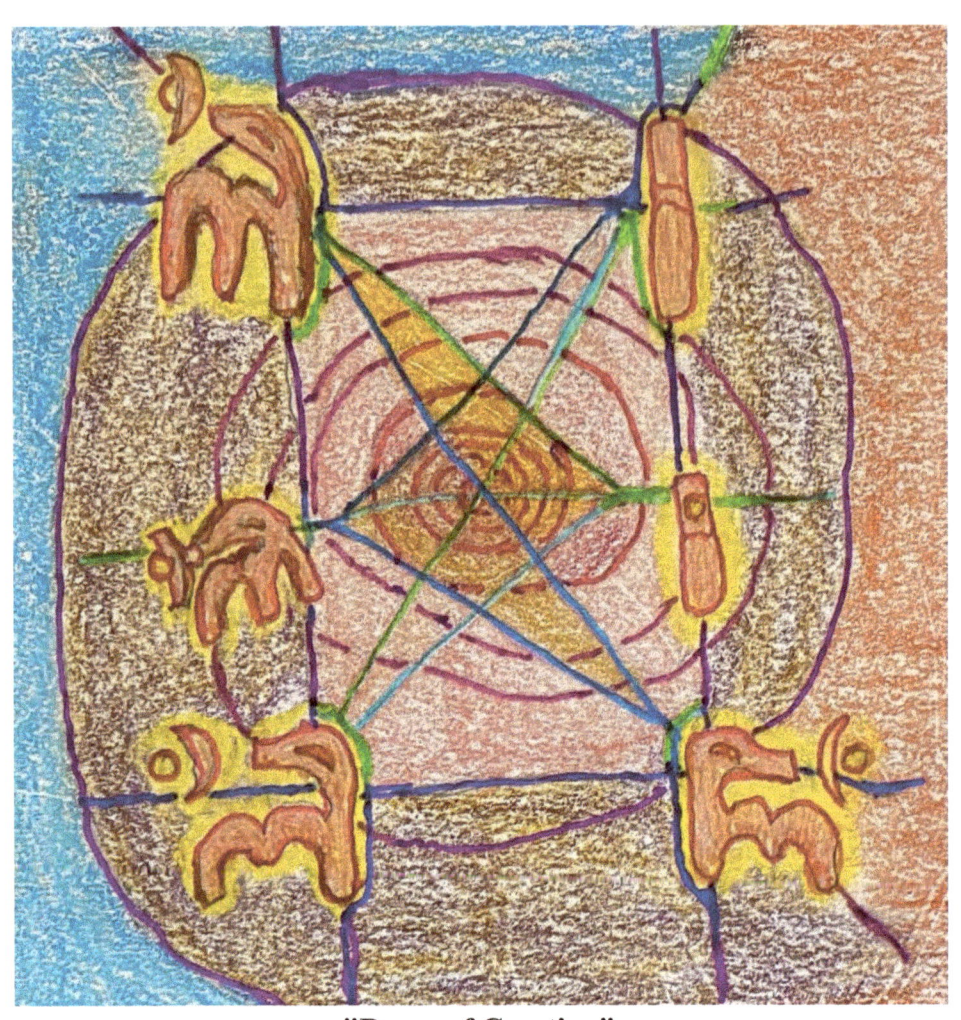

"Dawn of Creation"

Mandalas, 72

30. "Dawn of Creation."

This mandala represents the moment of creation, with life bursting forth from what Gregory of Nazianzus called "the Abyss of the Father."

Life's purpose exists from the moment of beginning.

Life's Creator abides among those created.

Life's destination is a return to the fathomless depths of its Author and Source.

Mandalas, 73

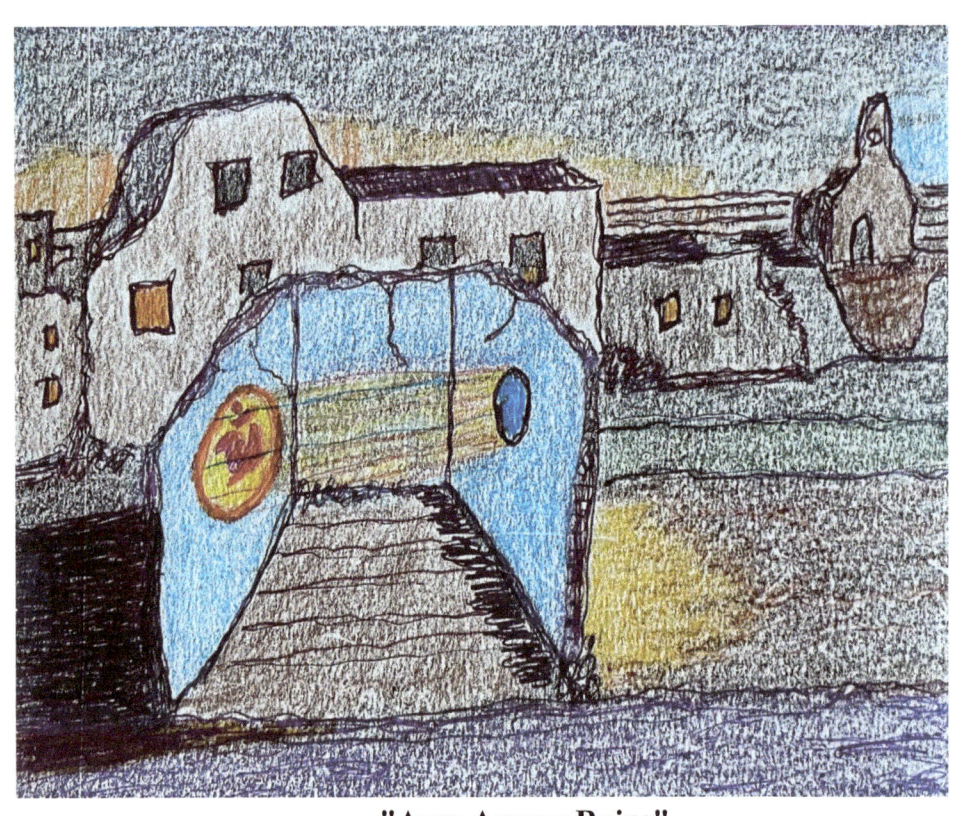

"Aum Among Ruins"

Mandalas, 74

31. "Aum Among Ruins."

We humans often assume that the way we've seen things done is the "right" way. We suspect that what differs is wrong, perhaps profoundly so.

This mandala, however, represents an alternate reality. Across human experience, from what we consider the least to the most advanced, we have sought to understand our place in the universe. We have sought communion in a fearsome world with One who might be our relief and consolation in it.

Something in us longs for this to be so, even if at times we cannot bring ourselves to believe it. This mandala represents those earliest holy places, built by those seeking a redeeming God.

Forms of worship, names for the holy, and other details differ. In places, the sweep of time shows clearly that much of the ancient form was brutal, barbaric. Yet when we look at our own traditions soberly, we see the same.

Respect the longing in the human heart! Learn from insights that, though different from our own, shed light on the same infinite Source. Allow all to grow together, *"Till we all come in the unity of the faith, and of the knowledge of the Son of God, unto a perfect man, unto the measure of the stature of the fulness of Christ."* **Ephesians 4:13**

All such temples are ours, whatever name they bear. Love and longing make them so.

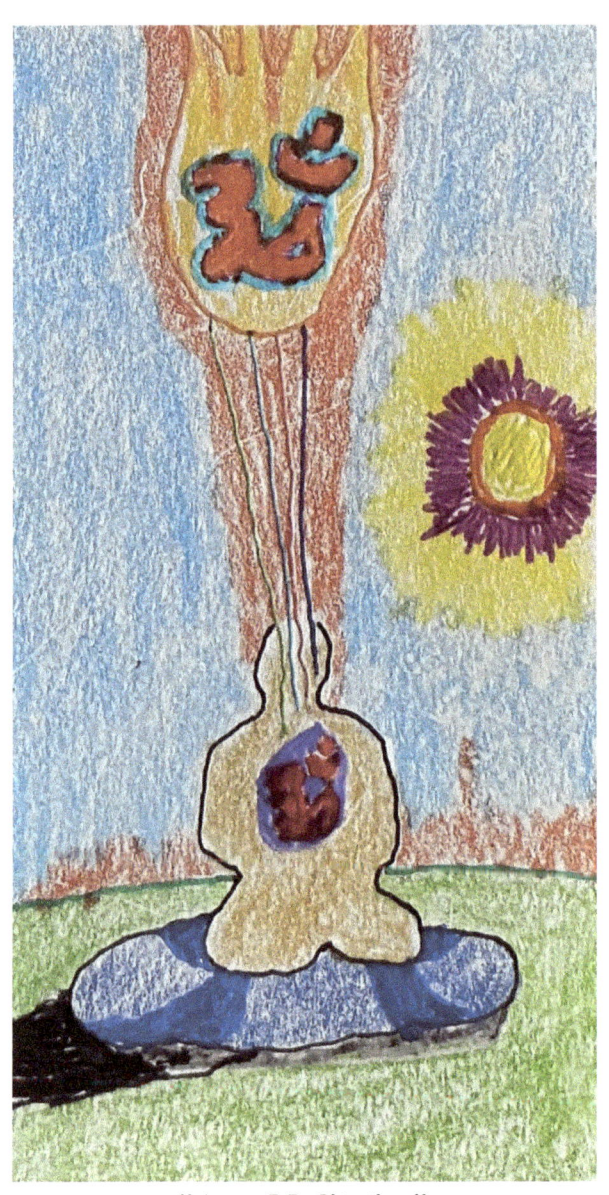

"Aum Meditative"

Mandalas, 76

32. "Aum Meditative."

This mandala represents humanity's age-old effort to realize the Ultimate.

The human sits in meditation, in prayer, all efforts focused on that reality from which all else springs, attempting to capture it in the depth of the soul.

He or she makes some progress. As we can see, though, what takes shape inside is not quite that which is sought. Our efforts fall short.

Can anything be done about this? Can a finite mind ever adequately know an infinite reality?

Unaided, the safest answer is No. Either grace will help, or the venture fails.

Where can such grace be found?

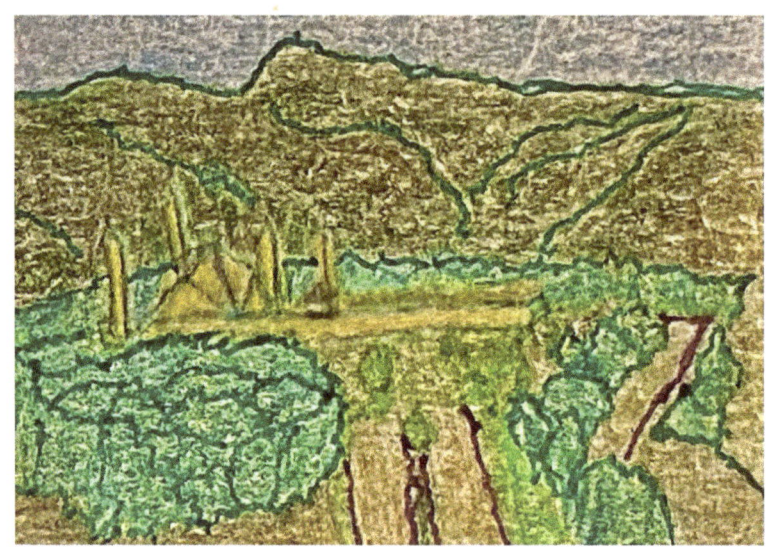

"King Faisal Mosque
Islamabad, Pakistan."

33. "A Temple."

Swami Vivekananda says this of temples and places of worship in <u>Practical Vedanta</u>.

"'Here is the symbol of fire,' they said. 'Very good! But here is another symbol, the earth. What a grand, great symbol! Here is this little temple, but the whole universe is a temple; a man can worship anywhere. There are the peculiar figures that men draw on the earth, and there are the altars, but here is the greatest of altars, the living, conscious human body, and to worship at this altar is far higher than the worship of dead symbols.

"The moment I have realized God sitting in the temple of every human body, the moment I stand in reverence before every human being and see God in him — that moment I am free from bondage, everything that binds vanishes, and I am free."

Oh, that we all may worship in such a Temple!

Mandalas, 79

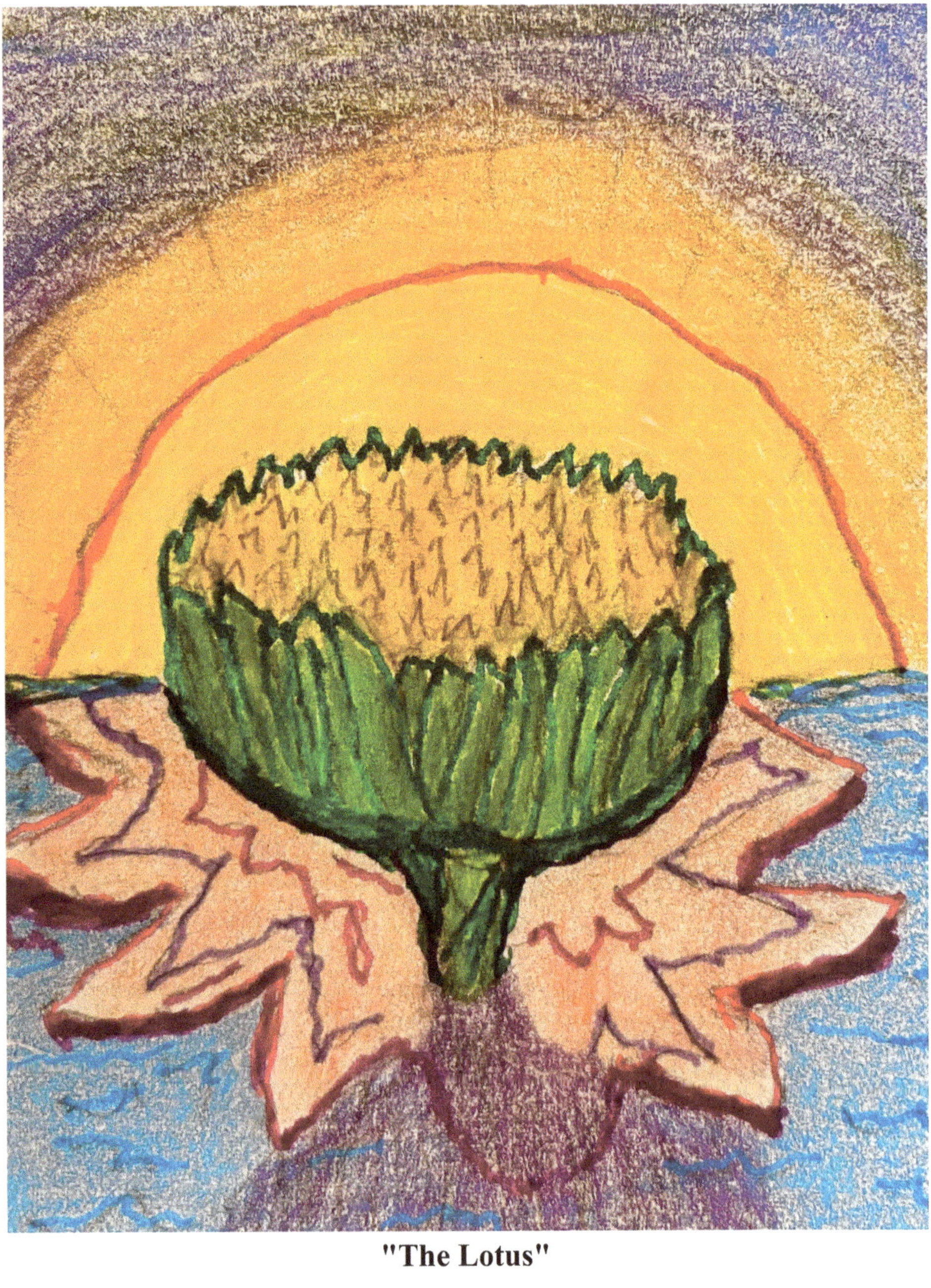

"The Lotus"

34. "The Lotus."

The lotus flower symbolizes truth in Buddhist art. Yet he lotus is noteworthy not just for its beauty. It is noted because of where it reveals its beauty: in the muck and mire, the filth and backwash of the world.

In places we would not choose to go, truth blooms forth. In the muck and mire of painful existencc, the unexpected beauty appears.

When pretty blooms appear clsewhere, we admire them. Roses in hothouses or sheltered gardens, are beautiful.

But the lotus blooms among the unwanted and defiled. Life drags us to such places, though we never choose to go.

Flowers grown in sheltered hothouses prove useless for our redemption and salvation. We need something that blooms even in sorrow, even in grief, even at the foot of a cross.

May we find the lotus of redeeming Truth blooming where we need it most!

Mandalas, 81

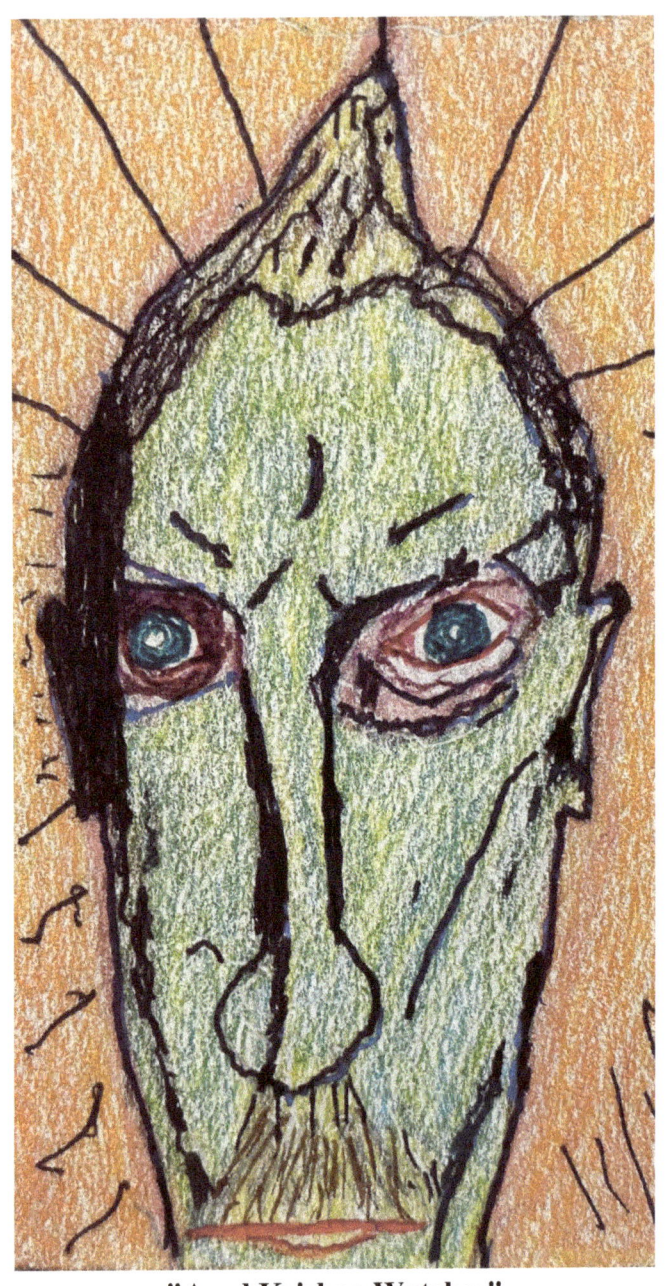

"Aged Krishna Watches"

Mandalas, 82

35. "Aged Krishna Watches."

Scriptures from many parts of the world contain stories of humans living impossibly long lives. Methusaleh in the Bible allegedly lived 969 years. Abraham endured 175 years. South Asian lore says Sri Krishna died at the age of 137, killed by a mis-aimed arrow.

Of course, we tend to reject those dates out-of-hand, or we take refuge in believing the way they were calculated was different. I understand, and would not want to argue about it.

For the sake of a deeper understanding, let's ask ourselves what such a long-lived perspective might be like. What would 137-year-old Krishna concern himself with?

In 137 years, he would have seen practically all that human life and nature has to offer. The rise and fall of kingdoms and powers would no longer surprise him. Passionate causes set forth as the world's salvation would no longer captivate him. He would long since have outlived fixations on pleasure and pain that mesmerize the young.

Would his concern not be for those who suffer, for those who lose hope? Would his concern not be to continue witnessing to a truth that redeems? Would his wisdom not lead him to a conviction that, though one may compromise on many things, one must never compromise on that Ultimate truth that is the hope even of long life?

If we could suspend our excuses for disbelief and look at the world through his 137-year-old eyes, what would we see? What would we value?

What would yet ring true?

Mandalas, 83

Mandalas, 84

Prayers and Meditations

Mandalas, 85

Beyond Fear and Worry

When a man
knows God he is free:
his sorrows have an end;
both birth and death
are no more...

that Supreme Divinity
who created
both Life and Matter,
who is the source
of all arts and sciences,
who can be intuited
by a pure and devoted mind;
realizing Him,
the blissful,
the incorporeal,
and the nameless,
one is freed from further
embodiment...

knowing Him who is
the origin and dissolution
of the universe;
the source of all virtue,
the destroyer of all sins,
the master of all good qualities,
the immortal,
and the abode of the universe;
as seated in one's own self,
transcending time
and form.

from Svetasvatara Upanishad

"Beyond Fear and Worry"
Svetasvatara Upanishad

Mandalas, 86

36. "Beyond Fear and Worry."

I crafted the word art for this prayer from Swami Tyagisananda's commentary on *Svetasvatara Upanishad*.

The opening lines of the prayer were an enormous help to me during a three month period in which I was fired from a job, forced to retire before I intended, and lost my father.

I invite you to memorize at least the opening paragraph and keep it close to mind.

Mandalas, 87

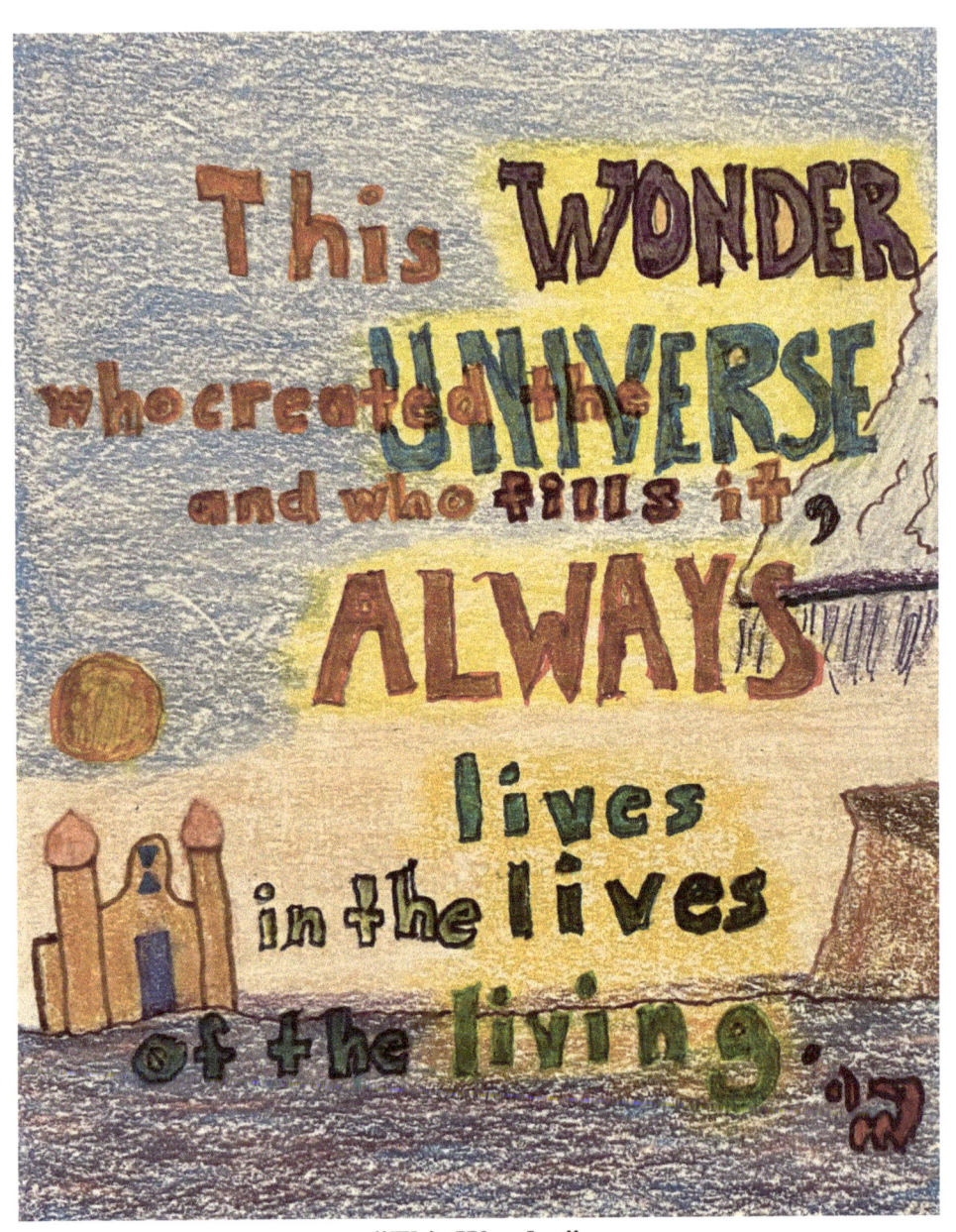

"This Wonder"
Svetasvatara Upanishad

Mandalas, 88

37. "This Wonder."

This piece of word art paraphrases the previous passage from *Svetasvatara Upanishad*.

This Wonder,
who creates the universe
and fills it,
ALWAYS
lives in the lives
of the living.

Mandalas, 89

¡DESCANSE, CISNE!

Cuando
conoce a Dios,
un hombre es libre.
Se acaban sus dolores.
Tienen fin ambos
el nacimiento y la muerte.

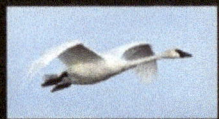

En esta rueda
enorme de Creación,
donde viven y mueren todos,
deambula el alma humano
como un cisne volando
sin descansar,
y piensa que Dios
está lejos.

Pero cuando desciende
sobre ella el
Amor de Dios,
entonces encuentra
su propia vida
inmortal.

Svetasvatara Upanishad

"Rest, Restless One!"
Svetasvatara Upanishad

Mandalas, 90

38. "Rest, Restless One!"

This Spanish poem also derives from the passage in *Svetasvatara Upanishad* cited in English in [Beyond Fear and Worry](). The swan, *cisne* in Spanish, symbolizes the human soul in South Asian symbology. I hope my non-Spanish-speaking readers will forgive my bias in favor of Spanish as a superior language for poetry.

When she knows God
a woman is free.
Her pains are over.
Both birth and death have an end.

In this enormous wheel
of Creation,
where all live and die,
the human soul wanders
like a swan
flying without rest,
and she thinks
God is far away

Yet when
the love of God
descends on her,
then she finds
her own immortal life.

Mandalas, 91

FUENTE DE TODA VIRTUD

ॐ

A conocer a Él
que es
el origen y la disolución
del universo,
la fuente de toda virtud,
el destructor de todos pecados,
el maestro de
todas calidades buenas,
el inmortal,
el hogar del universo...
como sentado
en su propio ser,
sobrepasando tiempo y forma.

Svetasvatara Upanishad

"Source of All Virtue"
Svetasvatara Upanishad

Mandalas, 92

39. "Source of All Strength."

This too is translated from the passage of *Svetasvatara Upanishad* quoted in Beyond Fear and Worry.

Aum
To know Him
who is
the origin and dissolution
of the universe,
the source of all strength,
the destroyer of all sins,
the master of all good qualities,
the immortal,
the dwelling place of the universe...
as seated
in one's own being,
passing beyond
time and form.

Mandalas, 93

As long as
the self
does not know
the Lord,
it attaches
to worldly pleasures,
and is bound;
but when it knows Him,
all fetters fall.

Svetasvatara Upanishad

"All Fetters Fall"
Svetasvatara Upanishad

Mandalas, 94

40. "All Fetters Fall."

One of the most vivid scenes in literature for me is the moment in Charles Dickens' <u>A Christmas Carol</u> when Ebenezer Scrooge sees Jacob Marley's ghost. Scrooge realizes that Marley drags chains with him, even in death. He asks why, and Marley tells him they are from his evil deeds in life.

Marley then tells him he has seen Scrooge's chains already prepared, and that they are even more grievous. This sets the stage for the rest of Scrooge's encounters in the story and, finally, for his repentance.

Both Judeo-Christian and South Asian traditions agree that our actions in this world forge chains for us in the life to come. As Robert Thurman, a leading Tibetan Buddhist scholar (and Uma Thurman's dad!) points out, believing that our individual selves end at death and that there are no enduring "chains" is wishful thinking.

If our hope is that dying will blot out our misdeeds, that hope is most likely vain. Our chains, forged by our attachment to pleasure, only fall when we know God to the depths. The Christian hymn, "Break Thou the Bread of Life" describes that moment in these words:

> Then shall all bondage cease, all fetters fall;
> and I shall find my peace, my All in all!

May that moment come for each of us!

Mandalas, 95

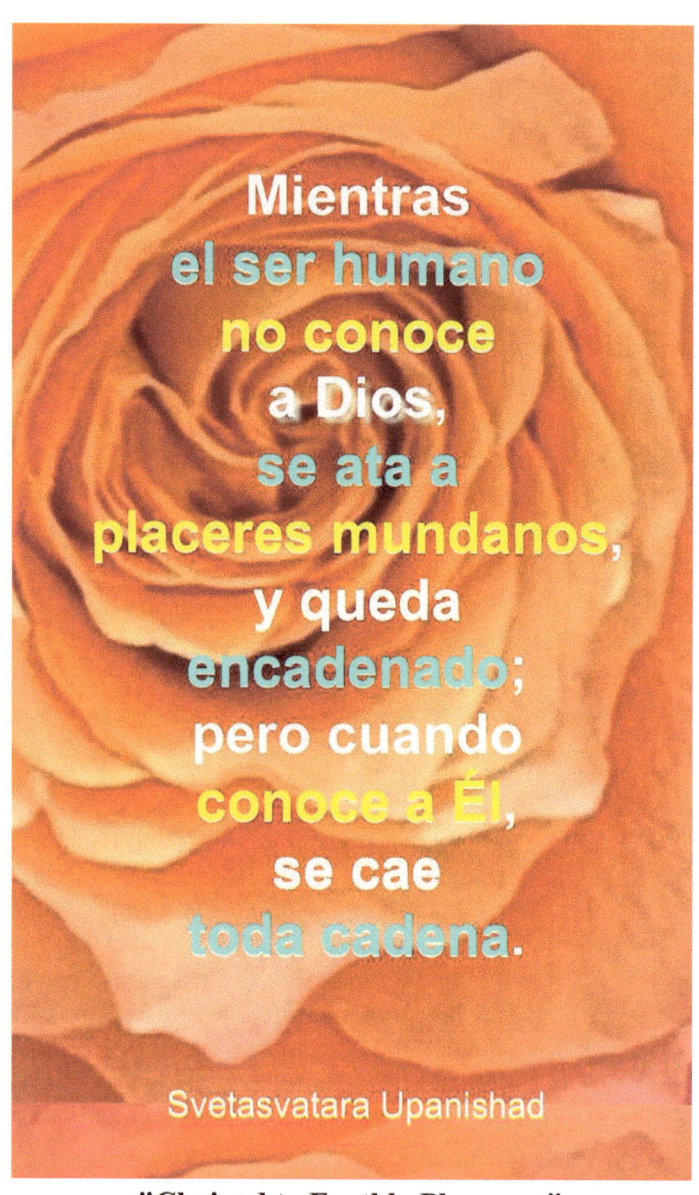

Mientras
el ser humano
no conoce
a Dios,
se ata a
placeres mundanos,
y queda
encadenado;
pero cuando
conoce a Él,
se cae
toda cadena.

Svetasvatara Upanishad

"Chained to Earthly Pleasures"
Svetasvatara Upanishad

Mandalas, 96

41. "Chained to Earthly Pleasures."

This poem translates the passage from *Svetasvatara Upanishad* found it <u>All Fetters Fall</u>.

> While the human being
> does not know God,
> she is bound to earthly pleasures,
> and remains chained;
> yet when she knows Him,
> every chain falls away.

Are you chained?

Embrace this moment to be unchained!

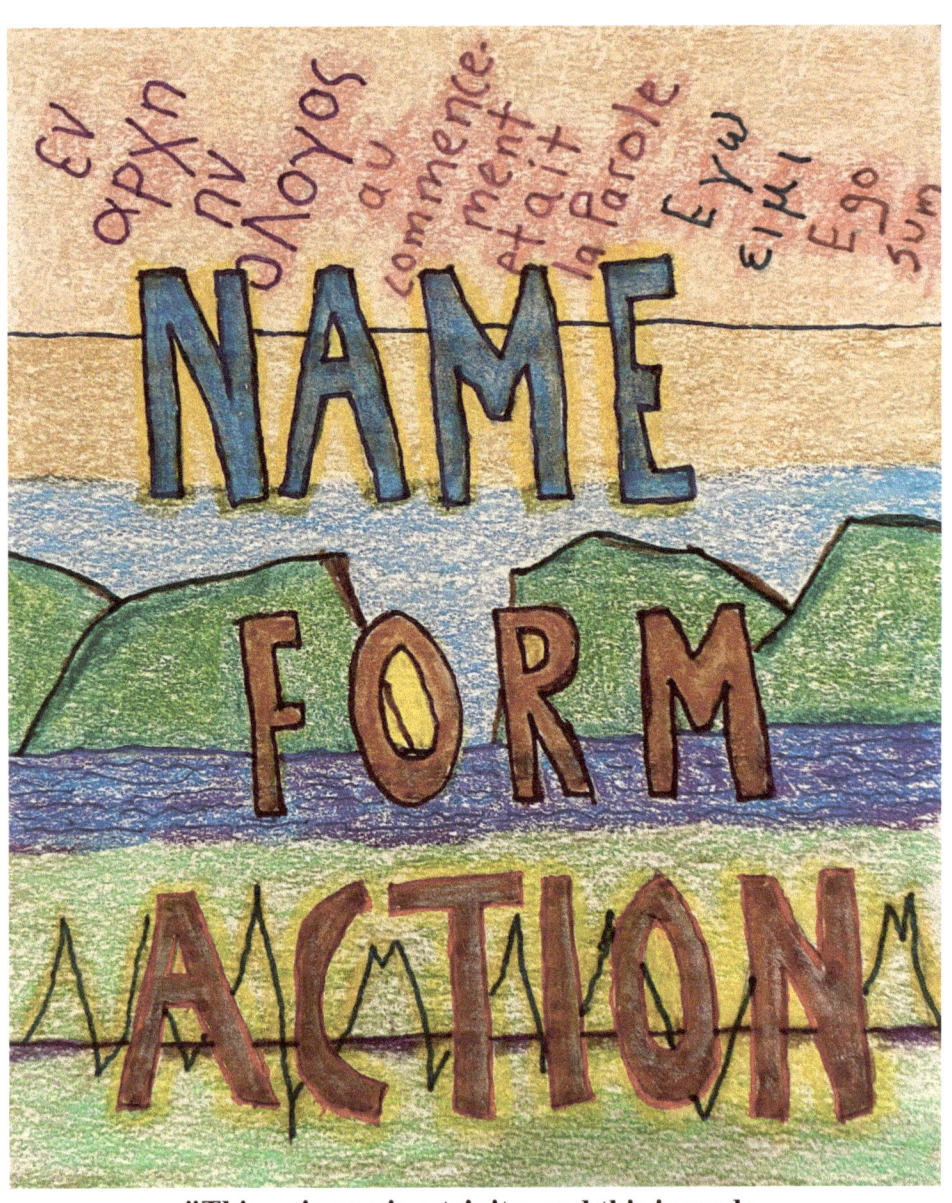

"This universe is a trinity, and this is made
of name, form, and action."
Brihad-Aranyaka Upanishad

Mandalas, 98

42. "Name, Form, Action."

Brihad-Aranyaka Upanishad teaches that "This universe is a trinity, and this is made of name, form, and action."

The trinity referred to is NOT the Christian trinity, but the universe knowable in part to its inhabitants.

Name, obviously, refers to the words and sounds we use to assign meaning and order to ourselves and the world around us. The "names" written above in the drawing mean "*In the beginning was the Word*" (**John 1:14**) in Greek and French, and "I am" in Greek and Latin.

Form refers to the physical structures currently existing.

Action is what is taking place as name and form interact. The entire universe is one action, seen correctly.

All three – name, form, and action – are constantly in flux. None endures without change. *Brihad-Aranyaka Upanishad* points seekers to an identity that doesn't change in the midst of it.

Mandalas, 99

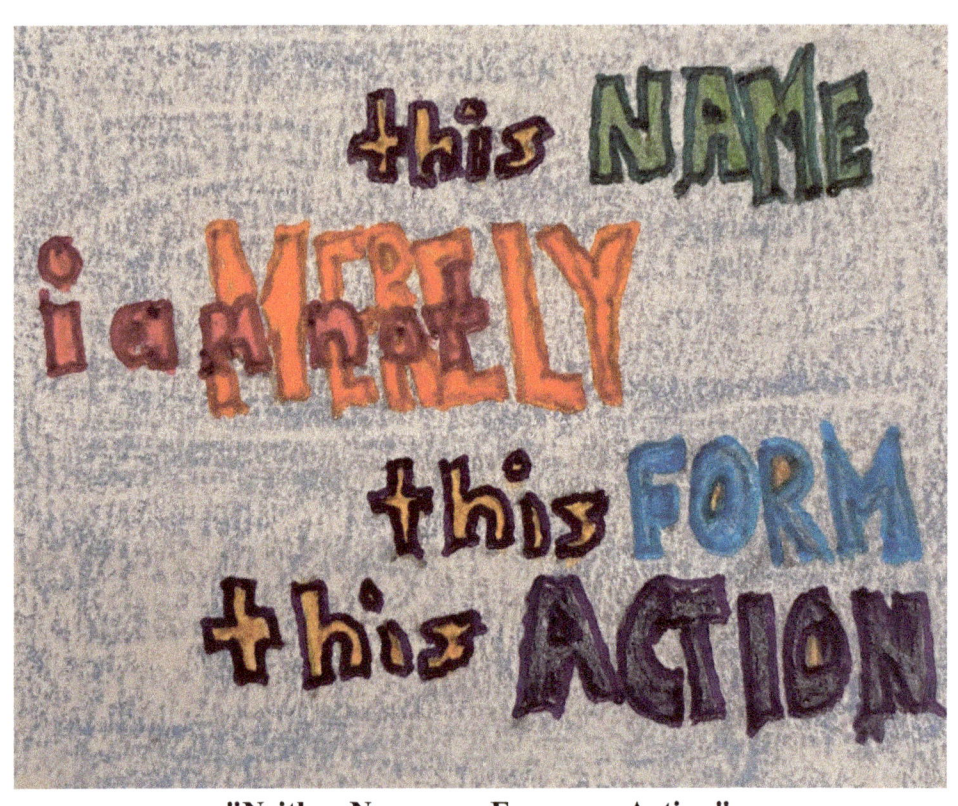

"Neither Name nor Form nor Action"
Brihad-Aranyaka Upanishad

Mandalas, 100

43. "Neither Name nor Form nor Action."

> "I am not merely this name.
> I am not merely this form.
> I am not merely this action."

Name, form, and action are the "trinity" of the material universe, as *Brihad-Aranyaka Upanishad* tells us in the previous mandala. We identify ourselves with those things from our earliest days of life. How could we not, when doing so seems so utterly obvious?

A central insight of South Asian thought, though, is that "we" are NOT anything we are aware of through the senses, Something, someone higher, ungraspable through the net of the senses, is the one aware of name, form, and action.

This mandala invites us to focus on that possibility. This is what Christians have called the *via apophatika*, the "way of negation." Understanding who we are NOT brings us closer to understanding who we are.

In that spirit, repeat the prayer above slowly, in the silence of your heart. We add the word "merely" in line with the Christian doctrine of Creation. A part of us indeed lives through this name, form, and action – but not the totality of who we are.

When this name, form, and action pass, as they unavoidably will, we need not suffer the agony of assuming they are all we are.

I am not merely this name, this form, this action.

What am I?

Who am I?

By meditating on Him,
by uniting with Him,
and by becoming one
with Him,
there is cessation
of all illusion in the end.

Without His grace
Release is not possible.
It is attained by him alone
whom God chooses.

For who can refuse
to be absorbed
in that ocean of Divine bliss
and infinite auspicious Divine
attributes and qualities,
if he has but the opportunity
of knowing them?

The universe is not a chaos
but a cosmos.

Narada Bhakti Sutras

"Not a Chaos but a Cosmos"
Narada Bhakti Sutras

Mandalas, 102

44. "Not a Chaos, but a Cosmos."

South Asian sage Narada wrote about something called "Bhakti", which later generations defined as loving God as a way of union with Him.

According to Swami Tyagisananda, "What is called Bhakti is nothing but the enjoyment of the Lord, the Master of the senses, with the senses themselves purified by intentness on Him, without laying any condition whatsoever.

"Bhakti is a loving sense of possession—a feeling that the Lord is one's own…"

"Bhakti is adoring service of Him that implies centering of the mind on Him, expecting no other gain here or hereafter…"

"And in its own intrinsic nature, Divine Love is nothing less than the immortal bliss of freedom itself, which comes unsolicited by the grace of God and by self-sacrifice."

Bhakti states directly the necessity of grace to our spiritual growth.

It also claims in one of the most comforting lines in the annals of human spirituality, that "The universe is not a chaos, but a cosmos."

Mandalas, 103

O glorious,
all-pervading Lord,
we worship you
by mere repetition
of your name.

"Mere Repetition"
Narada Bhakti Sutras

45. "Mere Repetition."

Buddha states in _The Dhammapada_ that, "The bane of prayers in non-repetition."

In contemporary English, that means our problem with prayer is that we don't pray enough!

The idea of repetition is unpleasant to many of our contemporaries. We crave the new, the changing, the up-to-date. But to condition our minds to stay rooted in the Ultimate requires making the seeking of it routine. That routine only builds through repetition.

The monks on Mount Athos are reputed to repeat the "Jesus Prayer" continuously:

> Lord Jesus Christ,
> Son of God,
> Savior of the world,
> Have mercy on me, a sinner.

The American Hindu scholar and teacher Ram Dass recounted reciting his mantra (a brief prayer) over and over again throughout the day.

The Apostle Paul taught us in **1 Thessalonians 5:17** to "_Pray without ceasing._"

Let us repeat the Lord's name, or His attributes, or a scripture in our hearts until it becomes second-nature. Let us do so until the process lays bare the point of connection between our own souls and the One who is.

Be counter-cultural! Habitually turn you mind at every conscious moment to the unchanging Source!

Mandalas, 105

Siempre

Él

es el **alma**
del **universo**,
el **inmortal**,
y suya es la **soberanía**.

Él

sabe todo,
llena todo,
proteja todo el **universo**,
el **Soberano** eternal.
No se puede
ningun otro
a **gobernar**
el **mundo** siempre.

"Siempre"
Narada Bhakti Sutras

Mandalas, 106

46. "Always."

He is the soul of the universe,
the immortal,
and the sovereignty is His.

He knows all, fills all,
protects the universe,
the eternal Lord.

No other can govern
the world forever.

Narada tells us, "A belief in the grace of God and in the possibility of escape from the round of birth and death with the help of God is the only qualification for the study of the *Bhaktisūtras* and the practice of Divine Love.

"Even a hard-baked sinner, if he comes to have unswerving love for the Lord, must be regarded as righteous, for he has decided aright....

"He should cultivate and preserve virtues such as non-violence, truth, purity, compassion, faith in higher spiritual realities, and the like."

A teacher named Sadilya teaches that "Every one, to the lowest-born, is eligible to follow the path of devotion; this is borne out by the long line of devotees; besides, virtues like non-violence and truthfulness and love for God are common to all."

Mandalas, 107

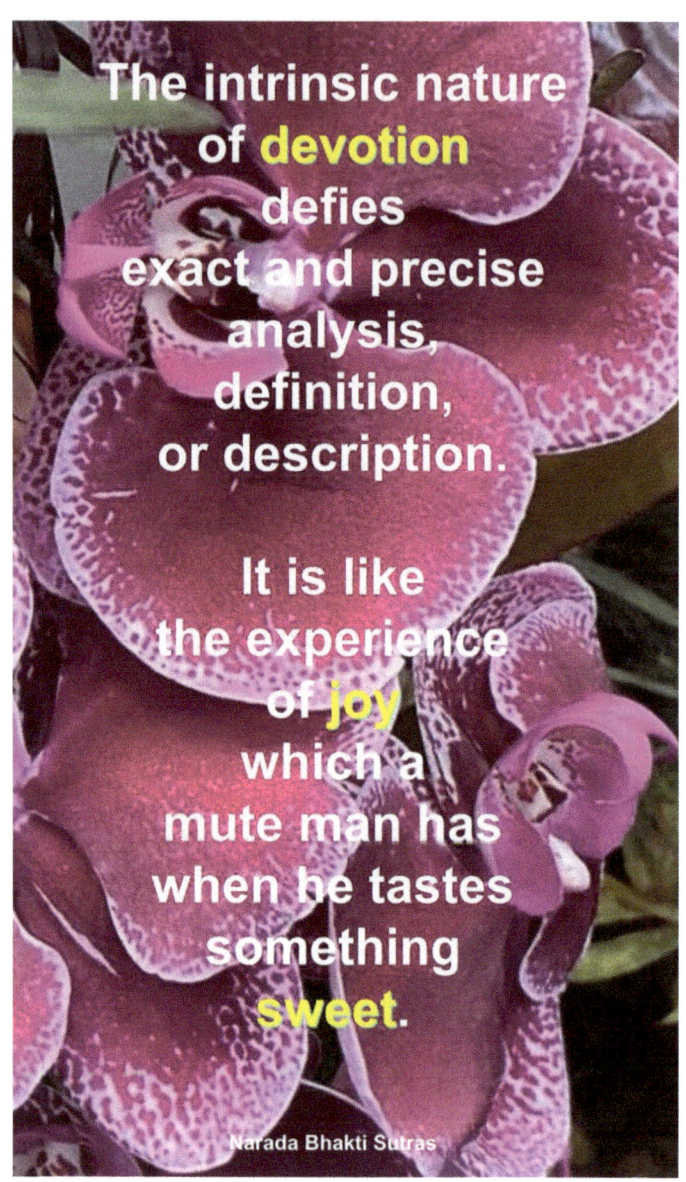

The intrinsic nature
of devotion
defies
exact and precise
analysis,
definition,
or description.

It is like
the experience
of joy
which a
mute man has
when he tastes
something
sweet.

Narada Bhakti Sutras

"The Mute Man's Eloquence"
Narada Bhakti Sutras

Mandalas, 108

47. "The Mute Man's Eloquence."

How can a someone unable to speak tell us the depth of his joy?

In loving God profoundly, we encounter something so lovely, so sublime, that even the wordiest of us is unable to put it into words.

As the Protestant cliche goes, such an experience is "caught, not taught."

My prayer for us is that we taste it, even if we can't describe it!

Mandalas, 109

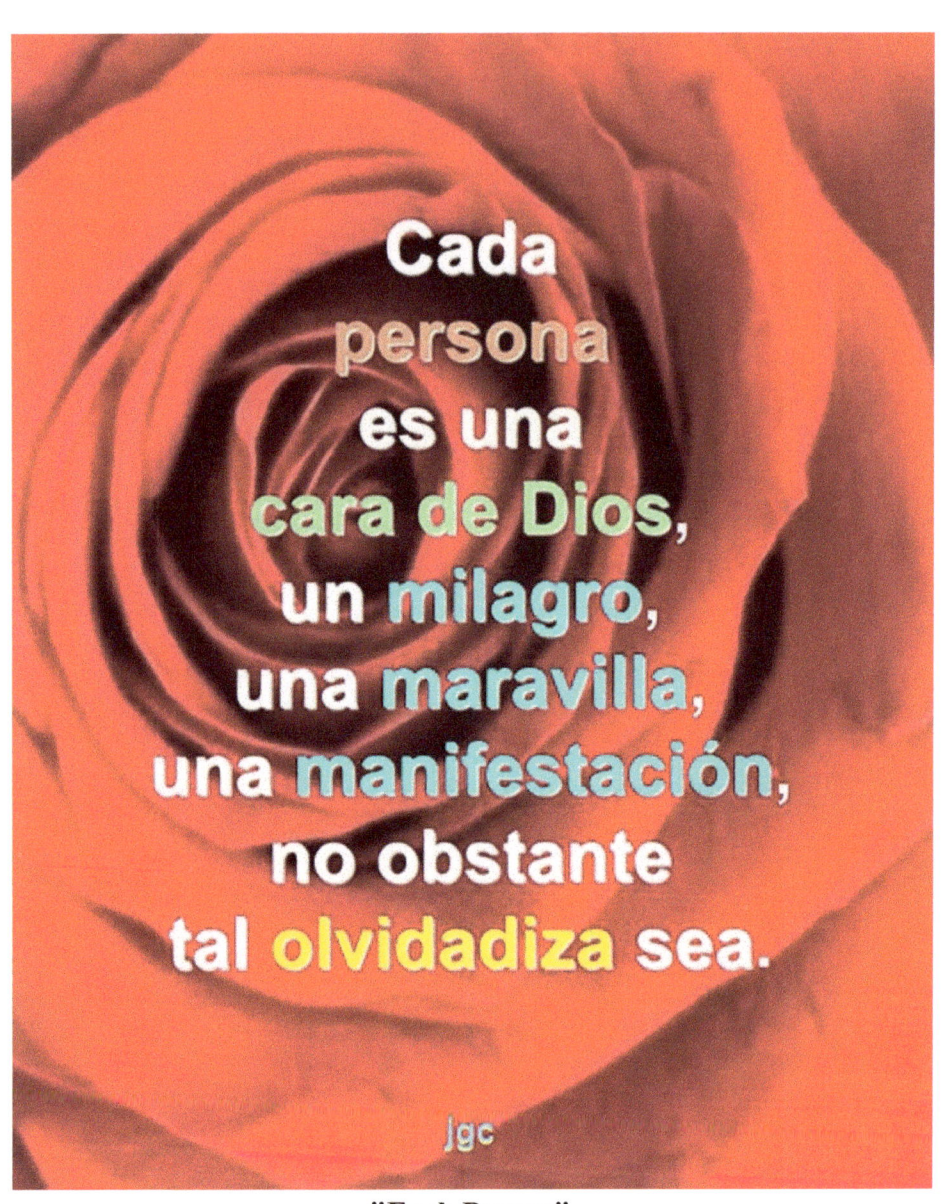

Cada persona es una cara de Dios, un milagro, una maravilla, una manifestación, no obstante tal olvidadiza sea.

jgc

"Each Person"

Mandalas, 110

48. "Each Person."

> "Each person
> is a face of God,
> a miracle, a wonder,
> a manifestation,
> however forgetful of it
> they may seem."

Sarada Devi, revered wife of 19th Century South Asian theologian Ramakrishna, said, "But I tell you one thing—if you want peace of mind, do not find fault with others. Rather, see your own faults. Learn to make the whole world your own. No one is a stranger, my child: this whole world is your own!"

The great Jewish teacher Philo of Alexandria put it this way: "Be kind, for everyone you know is fighting a great battle."

In our harsh, hyper-competitive world, coming to see others this way takes intentional effort. For me, that effort is especially hard in traffic. Yet unless I make progress in it, my peace is at the mercy of anyone who acts in a way I don't like. I am a hostage of things over which I have no control.

Can we do better? Do we have any choice? Patanjali taught, "Restraint does not come in one day, but by long continued practice."

Sri Shankara wrote, "It is obstructed desire that reappears in the guise of hatred and anger."

Let us practice of seeing others as a reflection of God. This is the better way.

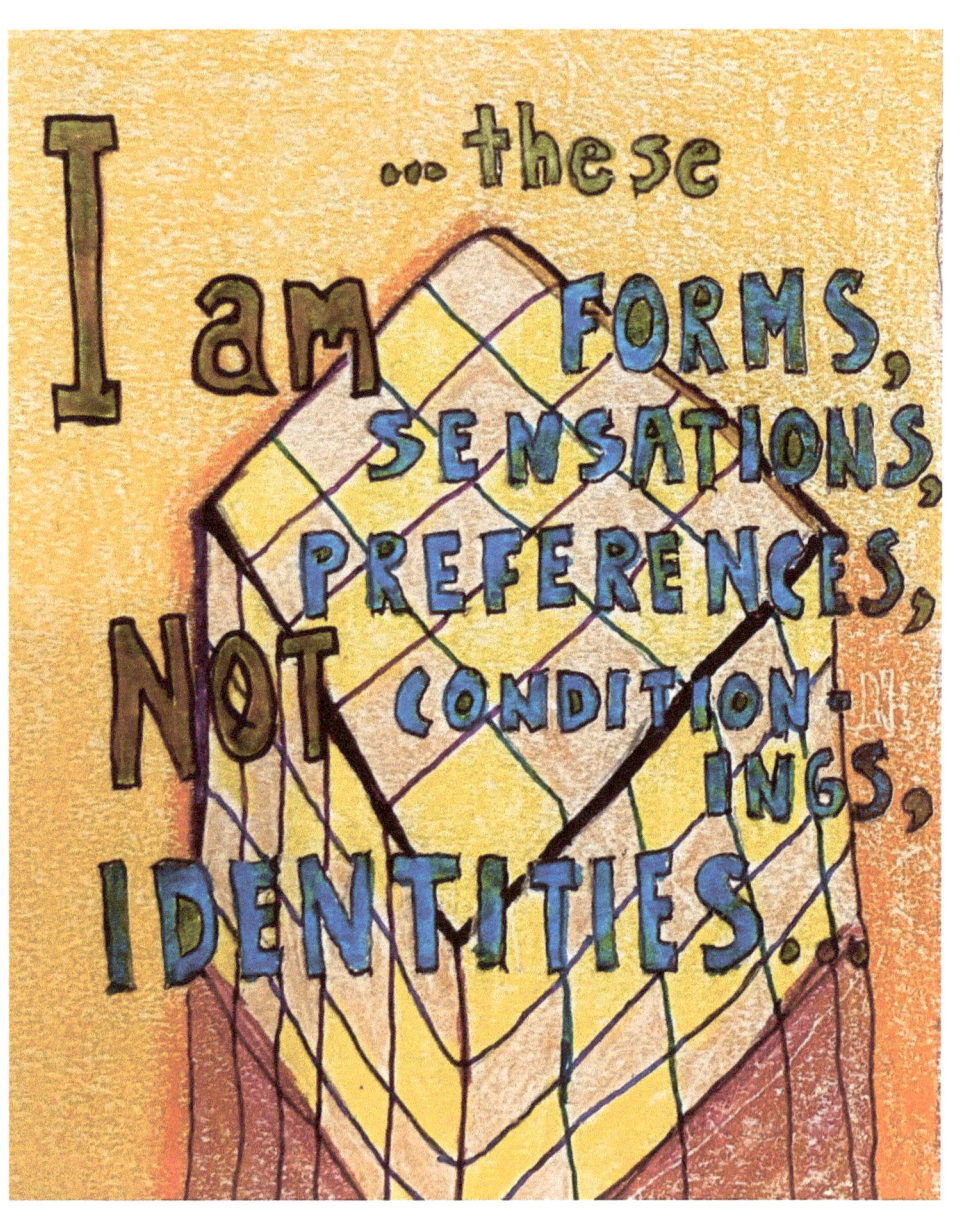

"I am not these..."
The Skandha Prayer

Mandalas, 112

49. "I Am Not These..."

Skandha in Sanskrit means "heap" or "pile". According to Buddhism, sensory experience can be broken down into five "heaps", five "piles" mixed together. They are form, sensation, preference, conditioning, and identity.

These heaps suggest a separate earthly identity underlying their existence in this world. This is an illusion, according to Buddhists. This mandala uses the same "way of negation" found in Neither Name Nor Form Nor Action.

Use these phrases as a meditation. Say the words to yourself slowly. Let their meaning seep in.

> I am not these forms,
> I am not these sensations,
> I am not these preferences,
> I am not these conditionings,
> I am not these identities.

You may add the adverb "merely" before the word "these" above, if needed.

Who are you apart from these heaps of experience?

Mandalas, 113

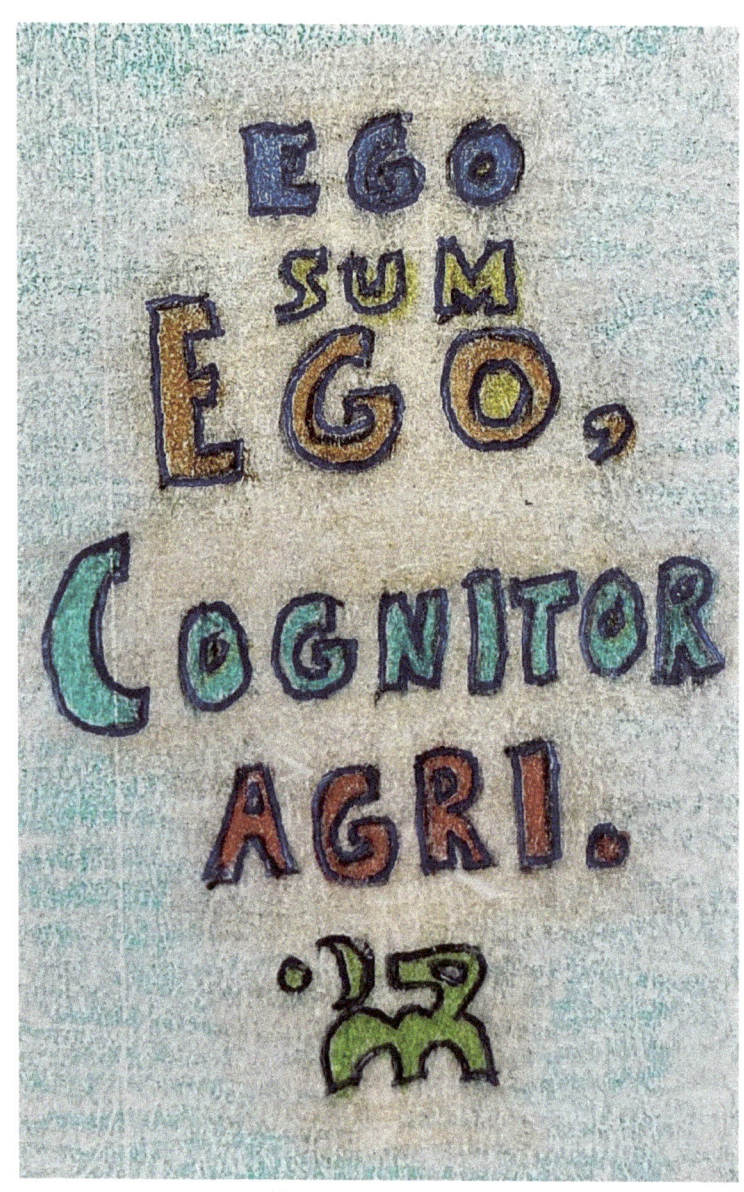

**"I Am t he Self,
Knower of the Field"**

Mandalas, 114

50. "I Am the Self, Knower of the Field."

This mandala answers the questions in the previous ones: Who am I? What am I?

This "I" is not merely a terrestrial identity, known to others. It is, instead, a great Mystery that neither science nor theology can answer fully.

An old (and somewhat dangerous!) meditation exercise is to ask yourself, "Who am I," then negate every answer. For instance, I might say, 'I am John Grady Cunyus.'

Then, I would negate that. 'No, 'John Grady Cunyus' is a sound heard with these ears, or letters read with these eyes, associated with a series of memories, preferences, and conditionings.'

That being negated, we proceed to the next, which is negated in its turn. The answer one comes to if the task is pursued to its close resembles something like this: "I am the Self, Knower of the Field."

Who is the Self? It is the origin, the beginning, the one perceiving, the Knower.

What is the field? The field is everything perceived, thought, sensed, remembered, and the like.

This is the answer. Yet knowing the answer alone without knowing the character of the One thus inferred may just be an empty exercise.

Who am I?

What am I?

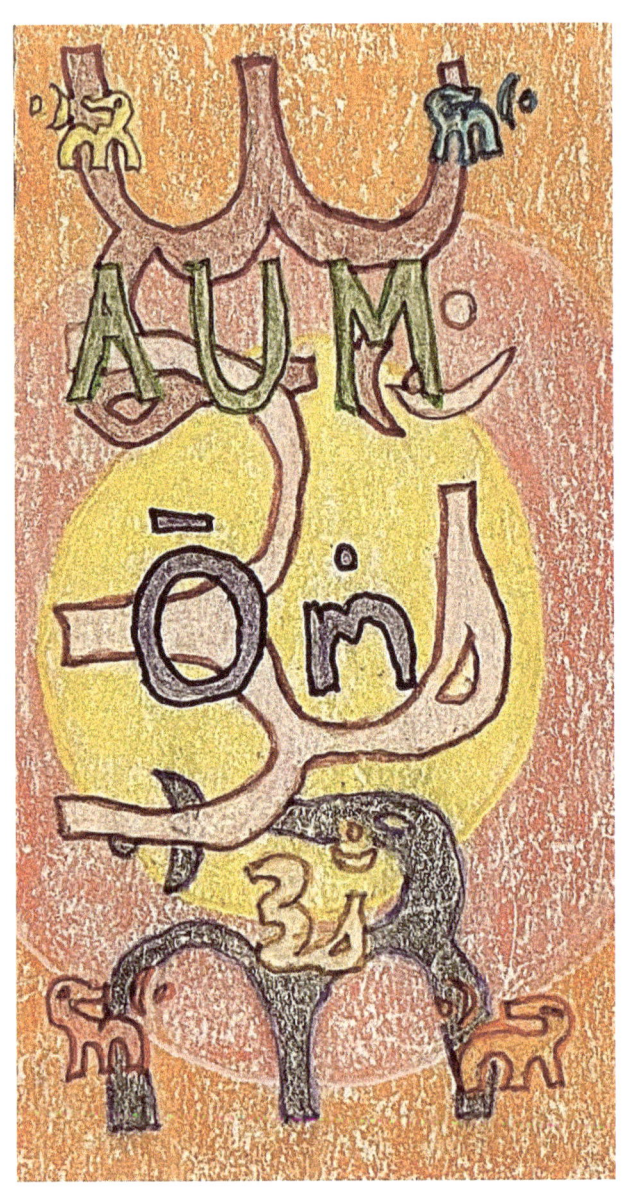

"Aum as a True Mandala"

Mandalas, 116

51. "Aum As a True Mandala"

This piece is a mandala in the truest sense, picturing the Aum emerging into the world, then drawing all things back to Itself.

Mandalas, 117

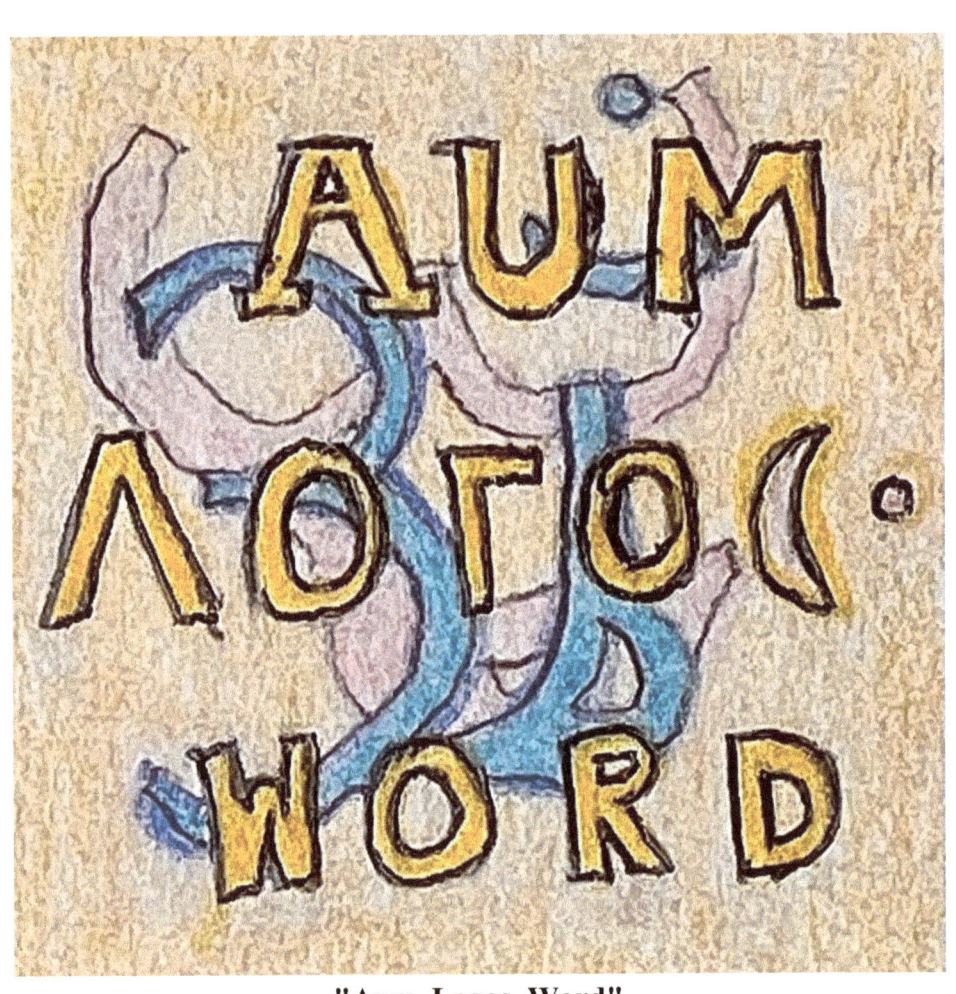

"Aum, Logos, Word"

Mandalas, 118

52. "Aum, Logos, Word."

This mandala expresses the deepest understanding I've found on this spiritual journey. One living Source is expressed in a multitude of different ways.

Here that One is expressed in four different languages.

Aum is Sanskrit, transliterated into English.

ΛΟΓΟΣ , *Logos*, is Greek, in the Koine vernacular of the New Testament.

Word, of course, is English.

 is *Devanagari,* the original alphabet into which the spoken language of Sanskrit was transcribed.

All of these different words and symbols point to the same Ultimate source of all that exists.

Mandalas, 119

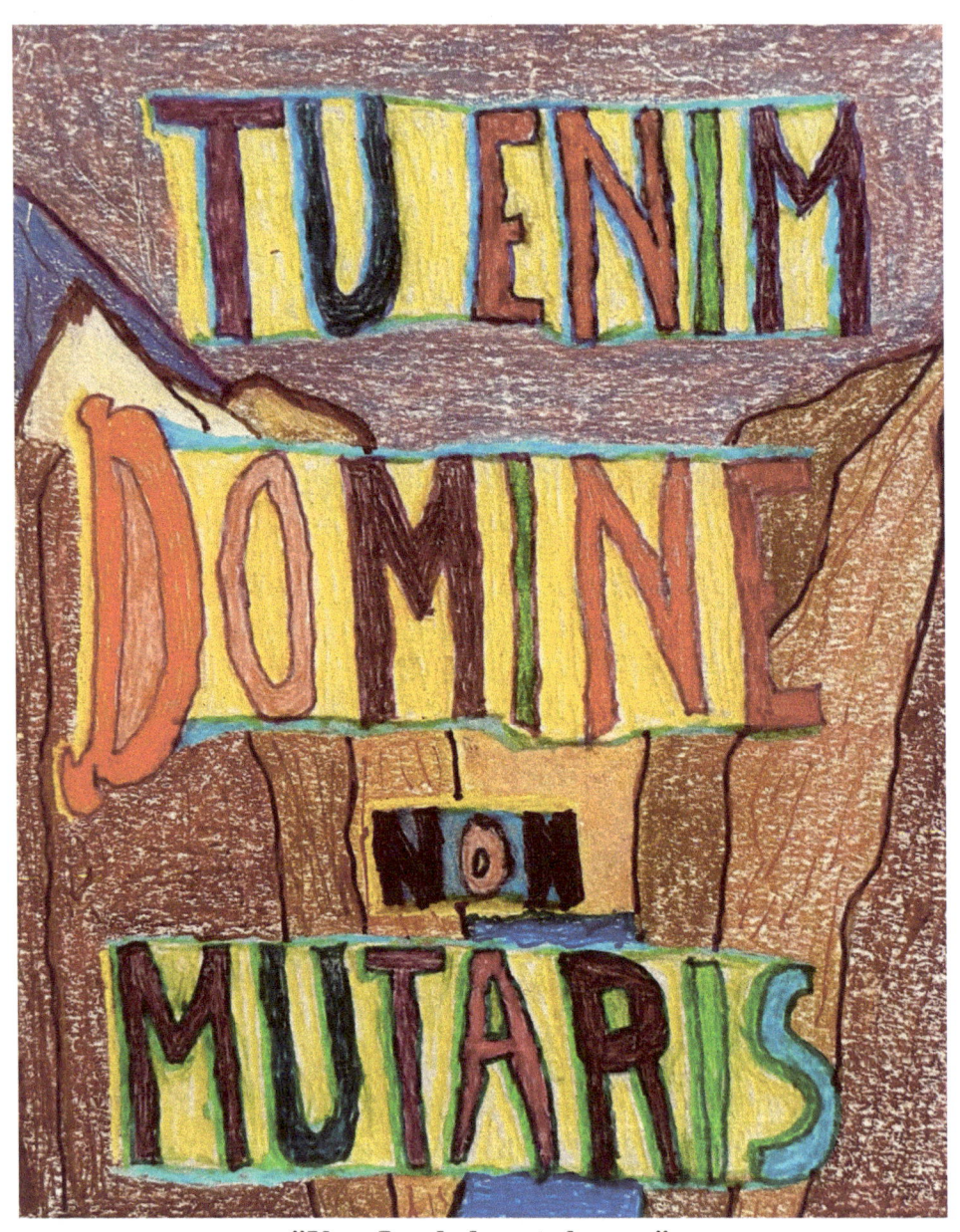

"You, Lord, do not change."
Adapted from Malachi 3:6

Mandalas, 120

53. "You, Lord, do not change."

Our possible growth in spirit rests on God's unchanging nature. This seems ironic: we change, the Lord doesn't. Yet without a constant frame of reference, how could we know which direction we were moving? And if dynamic grace were not among God's changeless attributes, our failure would be certain.

What do we grow toward? Ancient and medieval Christians believed in something called "the beatific vision" as the end state, glimpses of which are possible here. Cyprian, a Third-Century AD Bishop, said this: "How great will your glory and happiness be, to be allowed to see God, to be honored with sharing the joy of salvation and eternal light with Christ your Lord and God... to delight in the joy of immortality in the Kingdom of Heaven with the righteous and God's friends!"

The current Catechism of the Catholic Church tells us, "The beatific vision is when God, though transcendent, opens himself up to man and gives man the capacity to contemplate God in all His heavenly glory. Contemplation is the prayer of silently focusing on God and heeding His word; in other words, contemplation is the prayer of uniting with God."

It goes on to say, "The beatific vision, then, is ultimate union with God; indeed, it comes from sharing in God's holy nature via sanctifying grace."

Edward Pace, a 19th Century writer, defined the beatific vision as, "The immediate knowledge of God which the angelic spirits and the souls of the just enjoy in Heaven. It is called "vision" to distinguish it from the mediate knowledge of God which the human mind may attain in the present life. And since in beholding God face to face the created intelligence finds perfect happiness, the vision is termed "beatific."

Imagine being drawn close enough to "see" God, however that might take place beyond the realm of senses!

Mandalas, 122

MISCELLANEOUS

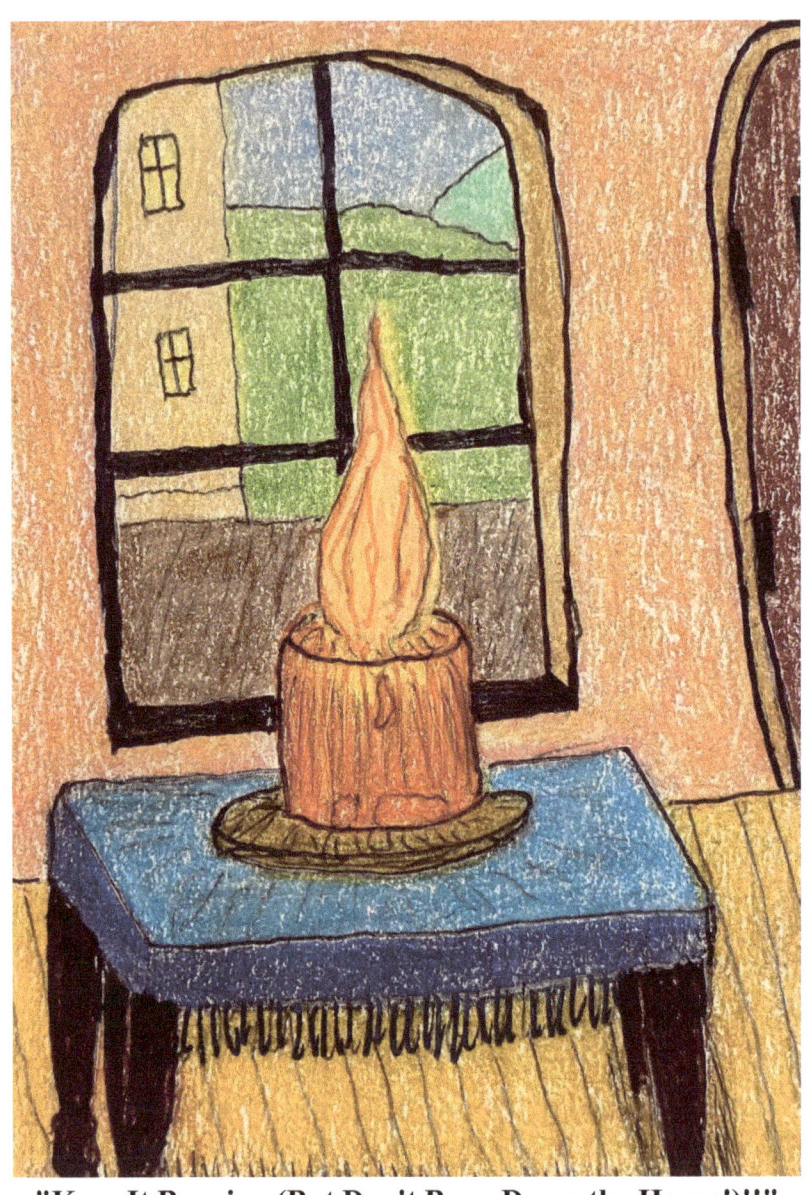

"Keep It Burning (But Don't Burn Down the House!)!!"

Mandalas, 124

54. "Keep It Burning (But Don't Burn Down the House!)!!"

Swami Vivekananda, credited with bringing Vedanta to the West in the late 19th and early 20th Centuries, says the following in his presentation of Patanjali's *Yoga Sutras.*

"Therefore do not hate anybody, because that force, that hatred, which comes out from you, must, in the long run, come back to you. If you love, that love will come back to you, completing the circuit. It is as certain as can be, that every bit of hatred that goes out of the heart of man comes back to him full force; nothing can stop it, and every impulse of love comes back to him."

Mandalas, 125

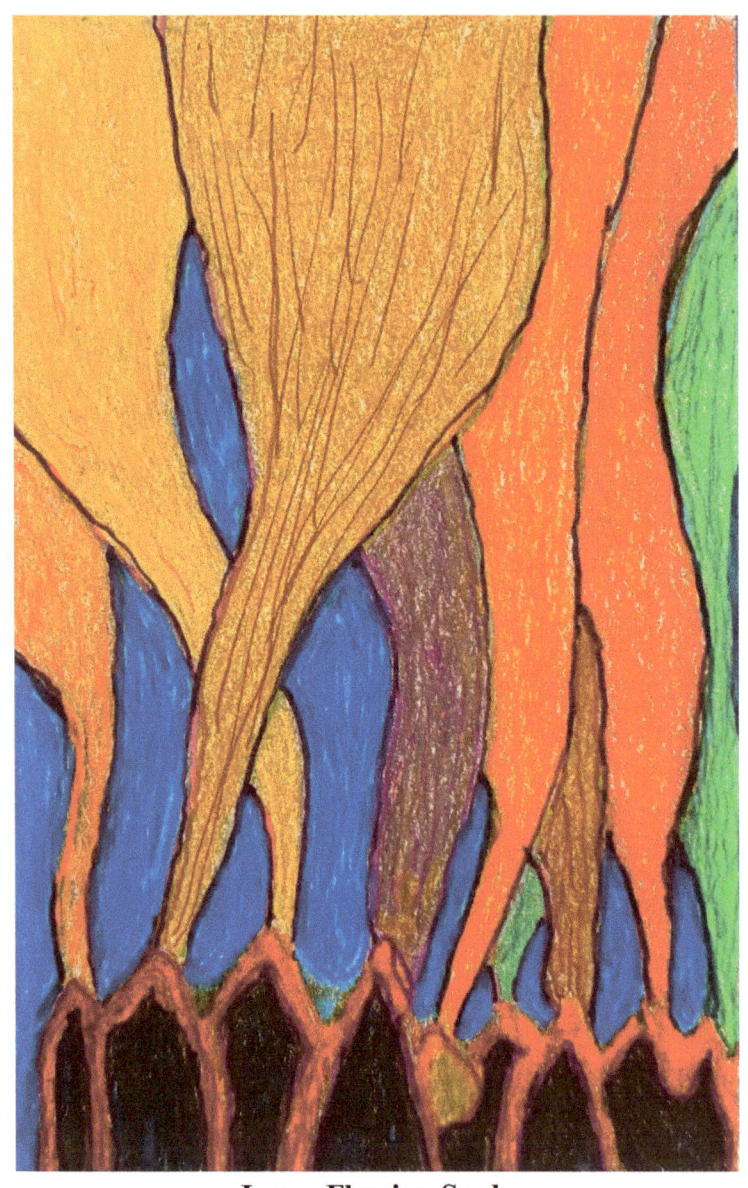

Long, Flowing Souls

Mandalas, 126

55. "Long, Flowing Souls."

Both Western psychology and South Asian philosophy agree there is far more to our individual lives than what we can see. We are connected to deeper realities, profoundly and irrevocably. Yet we focus on the surface and obsess over the superficial. Does that make us happy?

Swami Vivekananda said:

"We think of man, and see man as body. This is the great delusion."

Of God, he said, "One Teacher, Who is not limited by time, and that One Teacher or infinite knowledge, without beginning or end, is called God.

"The truths of religion, as God and Soul, cannot be perceived by the external senses. I cannot see God with my eyes, nor can I touch Him with my hands, and we also know that neither can we reason beyond the senses. Reason leaves us at a point quite indecisive; we may reason all our lives, as the world has been doing for thousands of years, and the result is that we find we are incompetent to prove or disprove the facts of religion.

"The most ignorant man thinks his body is the Soul. The more learned man thinks his mind is the Soul, but both of these are mistaken."

Mandalas, 127

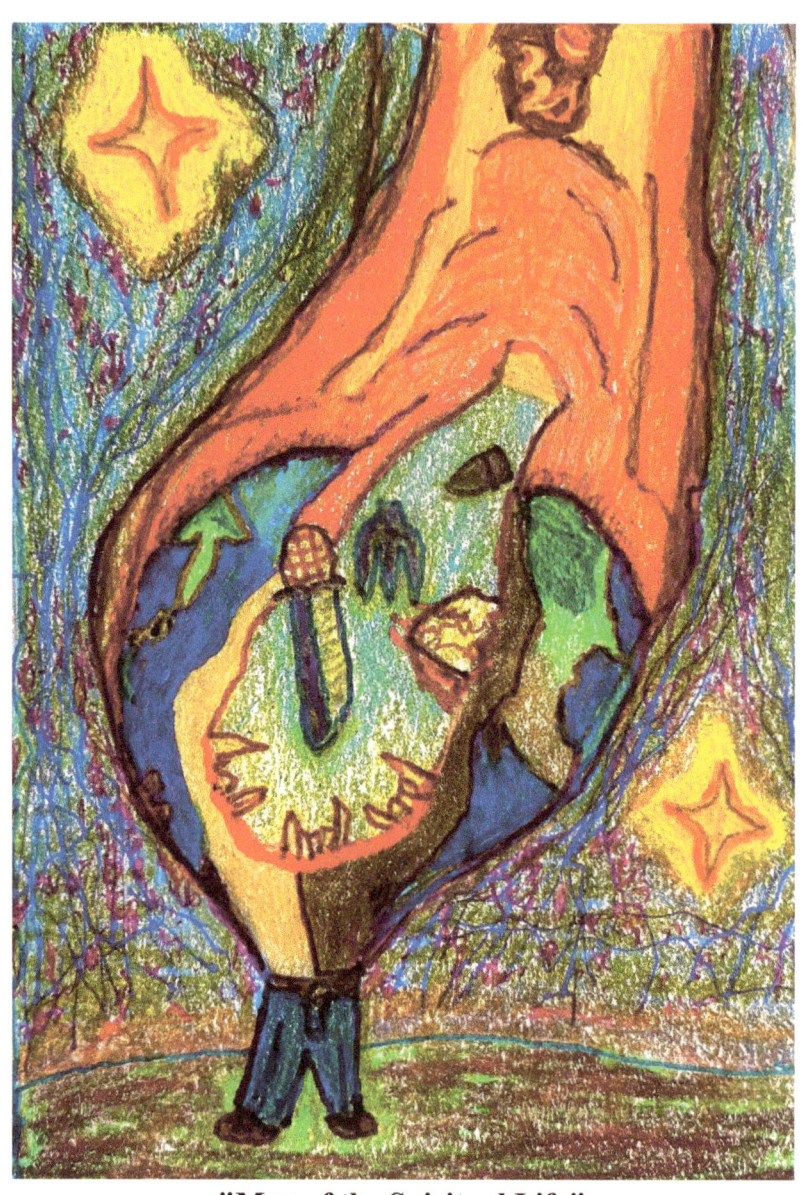

"Map of the Spiritual Life"

Mandalas, 128

56. "Map of the Spiritual Life."

This mandala shows that the spiritual life is not a stroll down easy street.

Jesus tells us in **Luke 9:23-24**, *"If someone wants to come after me, let him deny himself, and take his cross daily, and follow me. One who wants to save his soul will lose it. One who loses his soul for my sake will save it."*

It would be religious malpractice to say that living a spiritual life in this world was trouble-free. How do we balance living for God while stuck in traffic or sitting at a desk, while watching kids play soccer or doing all the ten thousand other things we must?

What do others say about our passion? What genuine opposition do we face when we no longer go along with our society's misplaced values? 'Why don't you care about money or prosperity? What harm can a little lying, a little rule-bending do? Why get bent out of shape on behalf of those in need? Ease up!'

Once that other life grabs hold, though, we find we can't "ease up." Like the Word with tent pitched among us, we are in it past the point of turning back. Jesus' words make it clear in **Luke 9:25**: *"What does it benefit man if he makes a profit of the whole world, but loses his soul, and makes a loss of his own?"*

Job says the following, plunged through no fault of his own into tremendous loss and sorrow, *"Though he slay me, yet will I trust him."* (**Job 13:15**)

That's the map of the spiritual life.

It is neither safe, nor safe to avoid. Then again, neither is life in general.

Mandalas, 129

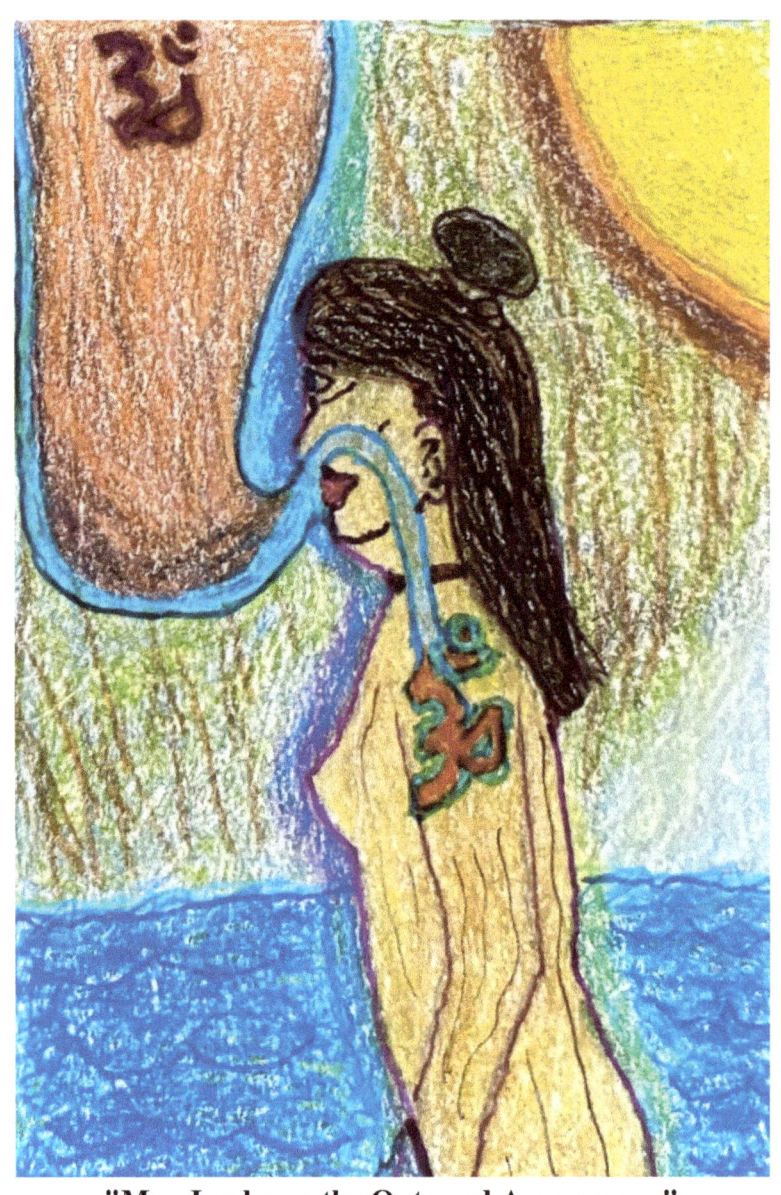

"Man Looks on the Outward Appearance"
1 Samuel 16:7

Mandalas, 130

57. "Man Looks On the Outward Appearance."

In **1 Samuel 16:7**, the Lord sends the prophet Samuel to find the person who will be Israel's new king. As he nears his journey's end, Samuel finds himself distracted by the outward appearances of those he interviews.

God tells him at that point, "*Do not look on his appearance or on the height of his stature, because I have rejected him; for the Lord sees not as man sees; man looks on the outward appearance, but the Lord looks on the heart.*"

I hesitated including this mandala because I am aware of that very issue. We, too, look on the outward appearance. We see a woman's shape. Outwardly, we might notice her face, her figure, her age. We might disdain her, lust over her, or judge her. Indeed, she may well judge herself the same way.

I'm too fat. I'm too thin. I'm too old. I'm too young. I'm too wrinkled. I'm not wrinkled enough. I'm too sexy. I'm not sexy enough. On and on, world without end.

Yet the Lord sees none of those things. The Lord looks "on the heart" – not on the physical heart, but on that innermost spiritual reality which is rooted in Himself. The Ultimate outside her is the same Ultimate inside her.

Part of growing in spirit is building the habit of looking beyond the outward appearance, looking to the heart itself. It takes practice, repetition, marked no doubt by stumbles along the way.

Yet we can condition ourselves to see this way, even though it flows against the grain of culture. Will we?

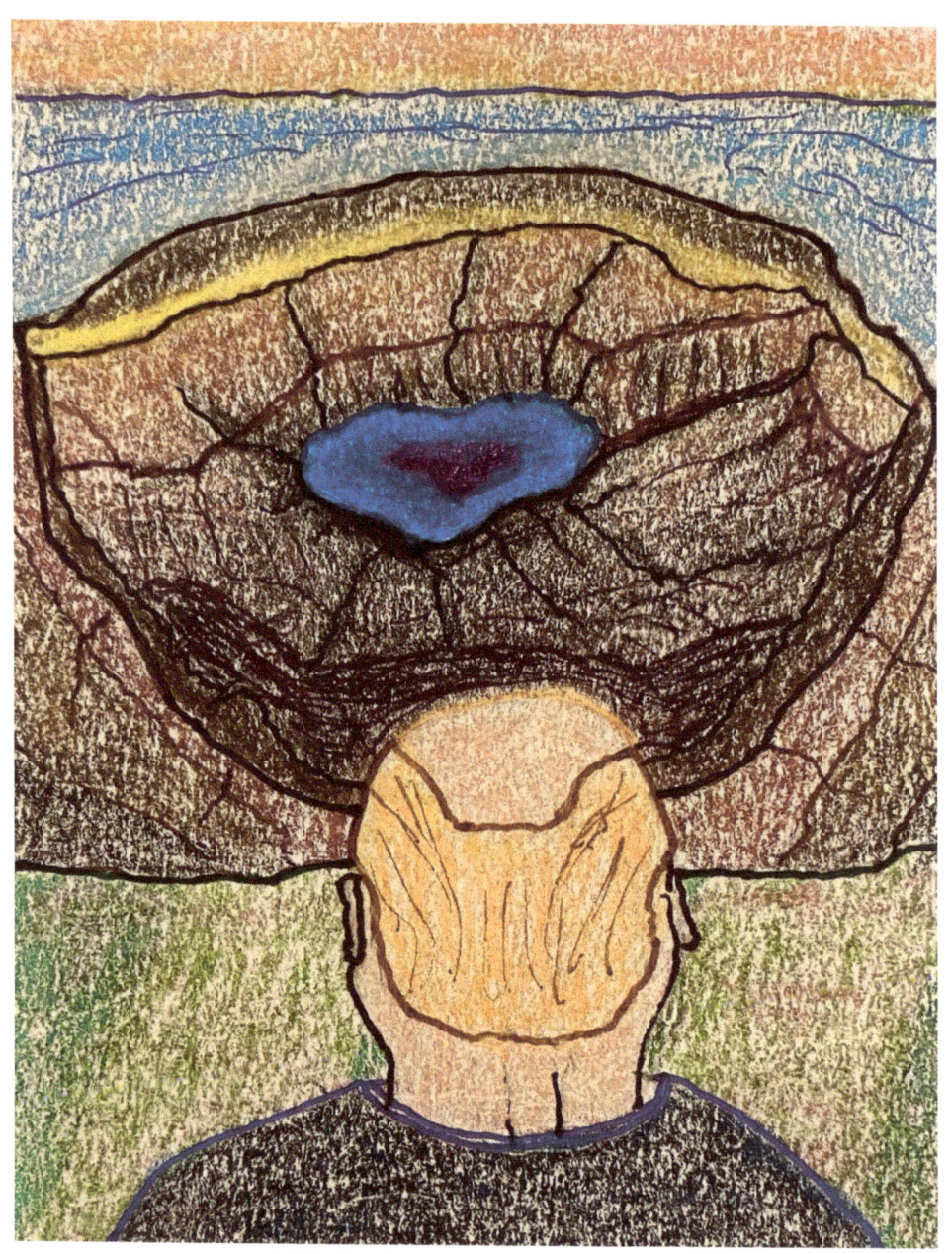

"Wally Stares Into the Abyss"

Mandalas, 132

58. "Wally Stares Into the Abyss."

Wally is "every man" and "every woman". The abyss opens before him in life. This may come as a surprise to him, since the broader culture does everything it can to avoid even seeing an abyss at all.

But Wally, "every man", has seen it. Now that he's seen it, something in him cannot look away. This is "where the rubber hits the road," as the cliche says. It's "fish or cut bait time" for Wally. What is his hope, if indeed he has any left?

I personally have relearned the crucial importance of admitting "I don't know" to facing the abyss in life. I don't know why the abyss exists. I only know that it's there. Friedrich Nietzsche said, "... if you gaze long enough into an abyss, the abyss will gaze back into you."

Wally may well wonder if there is any hope here? *Svetasvatara Upanishad* speaks of the dilemma:

> "If ever for man it were possible to fold the tent of the sky,
> in that day he might be able to end his sorrow
> without the help of God."

We are all Wally.

What is your hope, even staring into the abyss?

Mandalas, 133

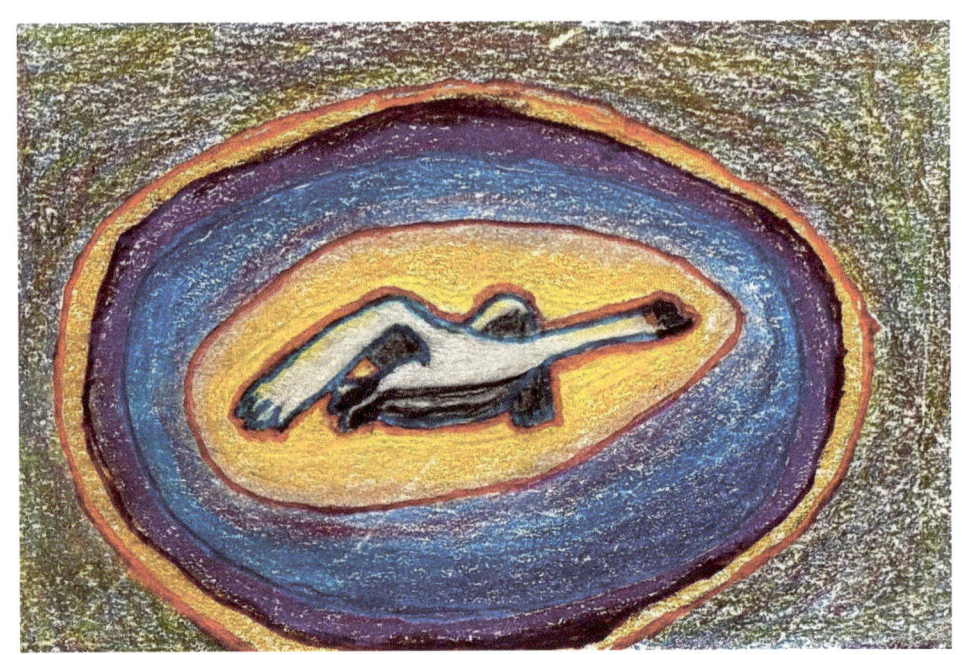

"The Human Soul"

59. "The Human Soul."

South Asian theologians compare the human soul to a swan, as we saw in the earlier mandala Rest, Restless One, Let us consider the comparison.

Once roused from its roost, a swan will fly great, restless distances looking for a safe place to set down. It makes its home once it lands, yet only until something startles it away. The long, restless flight repeats itself over and over.

Your soul has set down in this place, this body, this life, this world. Now, before something agitates it into yet another flight to yet another temporary home, look around. Look to the Ultimate. Find a rest beyond agitation while this opportunity presents itself!

The One who in love walked on the storm, whose unchanging nature is your deepest root, can be found here.

As *Svetasvatara* put it, "When a man knows God, he is free. His sorrows have an end. Both birth and death are no more."

There is no better "roost" just beyond the next round of restless flying. This is the day that the Lord has made.

Rest, swan! Then let that peace fill everyone and everything you know.

Mandalas, 135

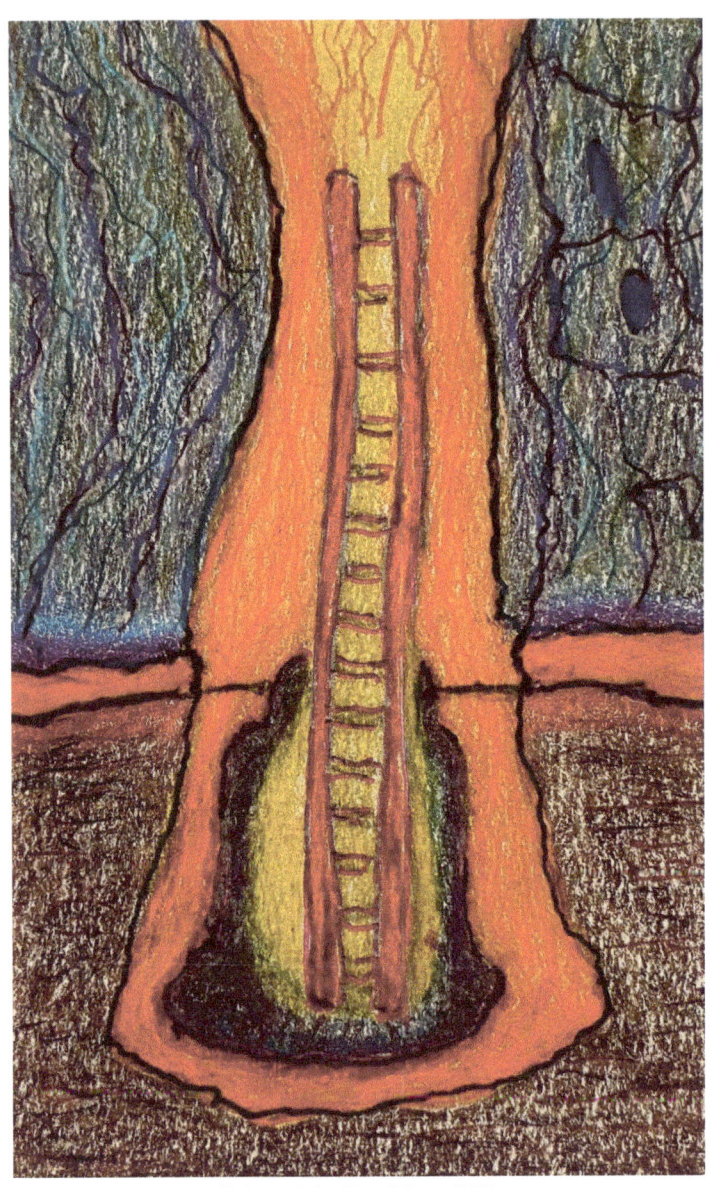

"Jacob's Ladder #2"
Genesis 28:12

Mandalas, 136

60. "Jacob's Ladder #2."

"He saw in sleep a ladder standing on the ground, and its top touching the sky. God's angels likewise were climbing up and down by it." (**Genesis 28:12**)

The ladder's still there.

Isn't it time to climb?

Mandalas, 137

Bibliography

The Latin Testament Project Bible
John G Cunyus, Translator
Searchlight Press, 2016
978-1936497294

Flames of Faith: A Thumbnail
Guide to the World's Religions
John G Cunyus
Searchlight Press, 2006
978-0595417674

A Path Beyond Suffering: Working
the Buddhist Method
John G. Cunyus,
Searchlight Press, 2008,
978-0964460966

The Upanishads
Juan Mascaro (Translator)
Penguin Classics, 1965
978-0140441635

Practical Vedanta
Lectures by Swami Vivekananda
Advaita Ashrama; 20th Ed. edition
(March 30, 2004)
978-8175050877

Svetasvatara Upanishad.
Commentary by Swami
Tyagisananda
Ramakrishna Math, 2022
Mylapore, Chennai, INDIA
978-8171205042

Narada Bhakti Sutras
Commentary by Swami
Tyagisananda
Ramakrishna Math, 2022
Mylapore, Chennai, INDIA
978-8171203291

Patanjali Yoga Sutra:
Swami Vivekananda's Insights into
the Path of Yoga
Commentary by Swami
Vivekananda
Namaskar Books. 2023.
INDIA
B0CLL1VVYL

About the Author

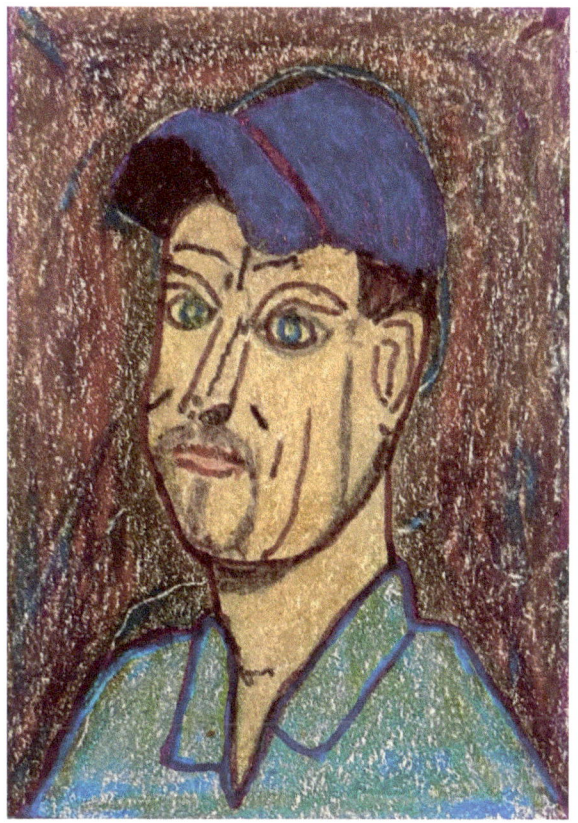

"A Portrait of the Artist."

Dallas, Texas, native **John Cunyus** spent thirty-six years in active ministry in Christian and Baptist churches. He authored dozens of books and articles, including The Latin Testament Project Bible, a completely new translation of the Latin Vulgate Bible into English. He carries on his ministry of prayer and communication now in retirement.

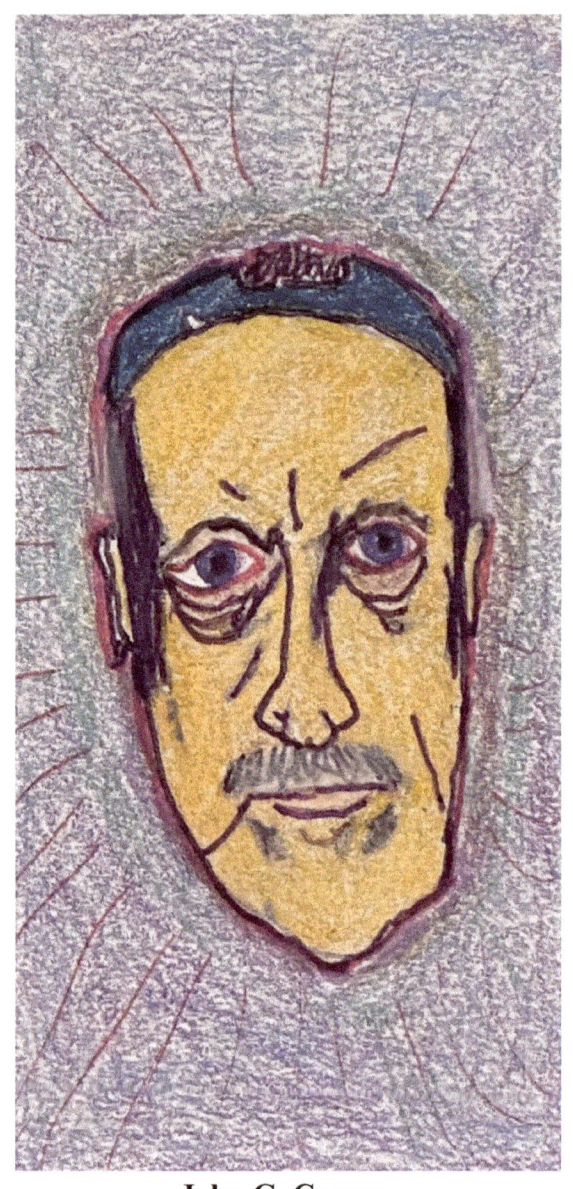

John G. Cunyus

Mandalas, 140

Also from Searchlight Press

THE LATIN TESTAMENT PROJECT BIBLE

An English Translation of the Vulgate

(Searchlight Press, 2016)

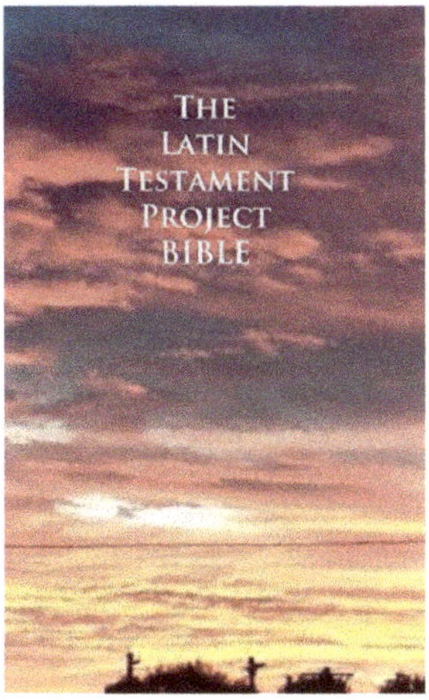
THE
LATIN
TESTAMENT
PROJECT
BIBLE

THE LATIN TESTAMENT PROJECT NEW TESTAMENT

A Latin-English, Verse by Verse Translation

(Searchlight Press, 2013)

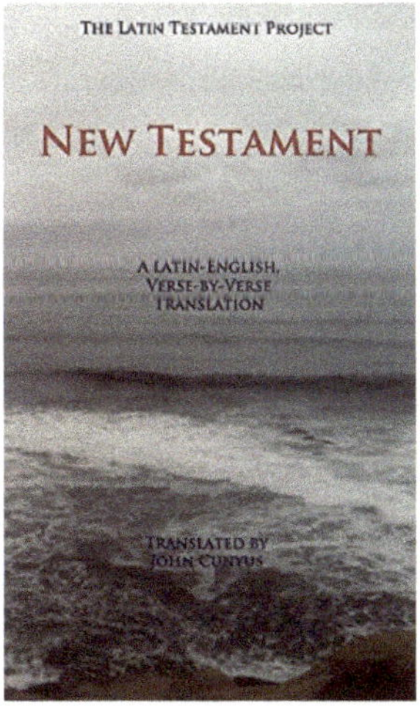
THE LATIN TESTAMENT PROJECT
NEW TESTAMENT
A LATIN-ENGLISH,
VERSE-BY-VERSE
TRANSLATION
TRANSLATED BY
JOHN CUNYUS

WONDERWORKING POWER:
A Fresh Translation of the Gospel of Mark
(Searchlight Press, 2011)

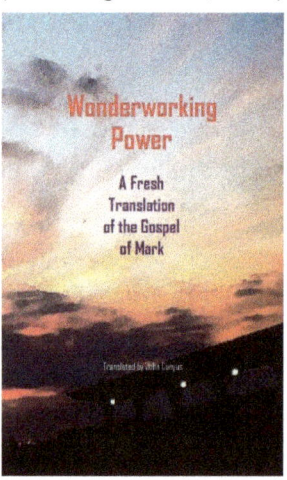

GOSPELS: MATTHEW, MARK, LUKE, JOHN
A Greek-English, Verse by Verse Translation
(Searchlight Press, 2017)

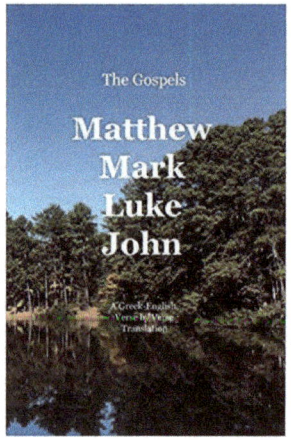

GRIEF RELIEF FROM THE BIBLE
A Workbook on Finding Strength
in Times of Loss
Searchlight Press (2017)

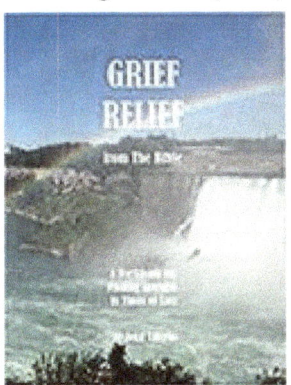

A PATH BEYOND SUFFERING:
Working the Buddhist Method
Searchlight Press (2008)

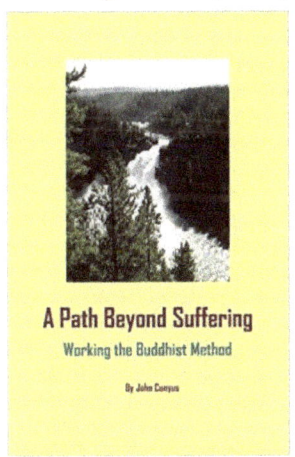

FLAMES OF FAITH:
A Thumbnail Guide to the World's Religions
Searchlight Press (2006)

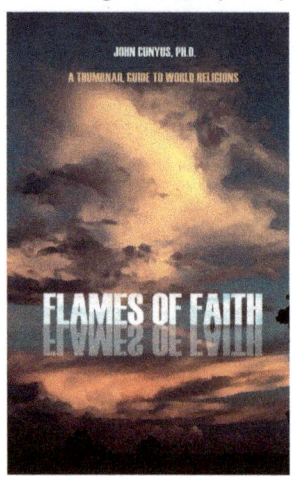

Searchlight Press
Who are you looking for?
Publishers of thoughtful Christian books since 1994.
5634 Ledgestone Drive
Dallas, TX 75214-2026
214.662.5494
www.JohnCunyus.com

Mandalas, 144

Printed in the USA
CPSIA information can be obtained
at www.ICGtesting.com
CBHW050353180724
11676CB00040B/1116